Singing
in Baghdad

*A Musical Mission
of Peace*

Cameron Powers

Published by GL Design,
Boulder, Colorado   USA

Singing in Baghdad, A Musical Mission of Peace, 2nd Edition

Copyright © 2003 by Cameron Powers
Manufactured in the U.S.A.
Published by GL Design, Boulder, Colorado, USA

All photos (including cover art) taken by Cameron Powers or Kristina Sophia and friends during travels described in this book.

Library of Congress Control Number: 2006920414
ISBN 978-0-9745882-5-4

Table of Contents

Preface	1
Introduction	3
Amman, Jordan	5
Aqaba and Southern Jordan	25
The West Bank and Ramallah	39
Colorado	47
Cairo, Egypt	49
Back to Aqaba, Jordan	65
Back to Amman	67
Into Iraq	77
Baghdad	81
Postscript	96
Historical Overview	99
A sea of E-Mail	103
Thanks	123
Cameron Powers Biography	124
Other Books by Cameron Powers	126

Preface

I first came into contact with Cameron and Kristina in late March of 2003 when I was living in Damascus, where I was studying Arabic and writing news articles. I had just returned from a week-long trip to Baghdad only days before the U.S.-led invasion.

I was sitting at an internet café, reading about the daily attacks on a once proud and defiant country, when I got an e-mail from Cameron. He had gotten my name from a mutual friend with whom I'd studied Arabic. In the e-mail, Cameron said he and Kristina wanted to go to Iraq. They'd heard I'd been there, and wanted some advice for getting in. I wasn't sure whether to laugh or be concerned that someone would want to travel to a country in the midst of an invasion. I responded to the note, saying that Syria had stopped giving visas because it (and I assume other countries) didn't give transit visas during wartime. I didn't hear from Cameron for several weeks after that.

Eventually, I got an e-mail from him saying that he and Kristina had gotten in by way of Jordan nine days after the entry of the U.S. Marines. I was relieved that they'd survived the war zone and surprised they were able to enter Iraq at all.

I met Cameron and Kristina in person for the first time in Damascus in the fall of 2003. It was during the Muslim holy month of Ramadan, and we had dinner, or "breakfast" as the locals would call it that time of year, at a bustling bistro in central Damascus. They told me they were trying to promote peace through music. I was intrigued, but not very hopeful about their idea. To me, this seemed too idealistic at a time when there were two wars raging in countries right next door to Syria. I didn't see how ordinary Americans could make a difference.

1

It wasn't until I saw them in concert that I began to see music as a possible way to bridge cultural and political divides – even during the hardest times. I enjoyed the concert, which was in Oakland, CA. I called an Arab friend on my cell phone during the concert, knowing he, too, would be impressed with the sounds. He was. And so was the American audience there that night.

The next time I saw the musical duo was one year later in Damascus, Syria. I went back there to write more news articles, and Cameron and Kristina went back to sing more songs. I introduced Kristina to a Syrian family with whom I had become close. When she told them she was a musician, they asked her to sing. When she began singing familiar tunes in Arabic, the entire room joined in. There was no longer any need for translations or explanations. Everyone understood each other.

Cameron and Kristina continue to surprise and impress me with their insatiable thirst for knowledge about and contact with the Middle East and their optimism at a time when there aren't many reasons to be hopeful about Arab-American relations.

—*Brooke Anderson*

Brooke Anderson is a journalist who has been writing articles from Syria since 2000. Her work has appeared in the *Lebanese Daily Star, Middle East International* and *Dow Jones Newswires.*

Introduction

More than two years have passed since the publication of the first edition of this book. During this time, Kristina and I have made two more trips to the Arab world. We have driven 40,000 miles through the United States, giving more than 160 *Singing in Baghdad* multi-media presentations to thousands of American citizens. We have been welcomed in more than half the American states by people hungry for information about Iraq and the rest of the Arab world.

Somehow it came to pass that I was an American who fell in love with Iraqi music and have learned to play it on my Arabic lute (an ancient kind of fretless guitar called an *oud*). For twenty years I have had many Iraqi and other Arab-world friends. When the U.S. government chose to invade Iraq, every ounce of my being was screaming, "No! Please don't do it! This is a new century and a new millennium and we can find better ways to deal with our problems and our perceived threats! We can no longer stand by and watch entire innocent populations being exposed to military violence. Those people are our friends!"

My internal scream was so loud that it carried Kristina and me all the way to Baghdad on a musical mission of peace. Others were feeling it, too. Testimony in the form of the hundreds of supportive e-mails we had received made that clear.

We have many things to learn from the ancient indigenous cultures still in place on Planet Earth. There are so many beautiful ways of being and relating for us to drink into our souls as we travel.

I cannot take credit for the journey described in this book. It is a powerful testimony to what can happen when we surrender both to fate and to our innermost instincts of compassion and love. As we can see, once this surrender begins to take place, a multitude of characters, every one of them a bright light, magically appears to guide us deeper into the mystery and finally out into the light of personal freedom. This is the kind of democracy that we pledge to live for. It is a democracy which knows no borders and requires no government. True freedom does not come at the expense of others. We are all in this together.

—*Cameron Powers, December, 2005*

Amman, Jordan

November 27, 2002

"You are the first English speaker I have ever met who speaks any Arabic!" our taxi driver exclaimed at 3:00 a.m., as Kristina and I traveled to a small hotel from the Queen Alia Airport in Amman, Jordan. Truthfully, my ability to speak Arabic is still very limited, but we can sing in Arabic, so we sang parts of four or five popular Arabic songs as we rode in the taxi cab.

The cab driver said, "I sometimes try to learn a little English by watching the American programs on TV, but all they ever show is bang, bang, bang, guns and violence. I like to watch romantic movies, not all that violent stuff. So I don't watch enough to learn much English!"

He explained that, because of Ramadan, the Islamic holy month, "We are not drinking liquids, eating, smoking or admiring the beautiful women now. We are fasting now."

"Ramadan karim! (Ramadan is generous!)" I said, as my friend, Souhail, had instructed.

At 4:00 a.m., five or six men joined us and we all sang more songs in the hotel lobby.

The elderly owner of the hotel exclaimed, "People all over the Arab world love to sing and enjoy. In fact, you could go to Iraq right now and be totally welcomed with your music."

"Let's go to Iraq then," I said.

We lay in bed as the sun was first showing light and listened to the call to prayer broadcast over dozens of loudspeakers outside our hotel window. "It's just the same as when I was last in an Arabic-speaking country, Morocco," I observed to Kristina. "These guys are bursting with emotional enthusiasm, and ready to sing at any moment." They all seem to live inside the same telepathic thought bubble! There is a tremendous uniformity of opinion about the basics, especially when it comes to hospitality.

Downtown Amman, Jordan, a city of refugees: first Palestinian, and now Iraqi. An old Roman theater is visible.

I spent the greater part of our trans-Atlantic crossing with my nose glued inside my Arabic language books and listening to tapes. It seemed to pay off; I was ready to enter into my first Arabic conversation with our taxi driver. Whenever I didn't understand what he was saying, I would just repeat his syllables to keep the ball rolling, and to teach my tongue how to make the sounds of the language. I went to sleep that morning with a big Arabic-speaking smile on my face.

Overwhelmed by a sense of impending catastrophe during the fall of 2002, I had finally lost all faith in being represented by the governments of the world. They all seemed to have forgotten that the majority of humanity wants peace. I came to the realization that we must represent ourselves. As musicians who know how to perform popular Arabic music, I realized that Kristina and I could represent the sizeable body of Americans who were not convinced that Iraq represented enough of a threat to justify an attack. We called ourselves *Musical Missions of Peace* and bought our plane tickets to the Arab world, in hopes that we could become people-to-people musical ambassadors. Little did we know that, for the next month, we would not see a single American tourist in Jordan and Palestine!

With news from all over the world available on the internet, it seemed the American government could not simply ignore the millions of anti-war demonstrators assembling all over the globe. I wanted people in the Arab world to know there were Americans like myself who felt a deep love and respect for Arabic culture. We knew that violent fundamentalists were but a tiny percentage of both the Islamic and Christian worlds, and I felt outraged to see the mainstream media demonizing the whole Arab world. They seemed to have a simple formula: publish only photos of Arab demonstrators screaming with anger, or photos of young Arab men being forced to their knees, handcuffed and placed under arrest. This way the world would eventually conclude that all Arabs are raging criminals. I had spent enough time in Arab countries to know that this was not the case. The reason, in fact, for publishing this book is so that people can see a different kind of picture.

During the second evening of our stay at the hotel, in walked Ali, the nephew of an Iraqi friend of mine in America. I had, in fact, known Ali's uncle for at least 25 years, and had learned my very first Arabic songs long ago with his help. I had called Ali earlier in the day from our hotel, suggesting we might go out for tea and get know each other. He agreed, adding, "You don't need to stay in a hotel!" Get your things and come over to my apartment." Kristina and I declined to come immediately, as we had promised our friends at the hotel that we would sing again that night. "Which hotel are you at?" Ali inquired. "I will come join you there!"

Soon Ali appeared and introduced himself. The singing had begun. Whoever was in the hotel lobby at the time joined in, as the songs we chose were among the most popular and everybody knew them.

We then went out with Ali for a meal which could have been called 'lunch,' since the sun had set as we had all broken the day's fast and so we were now ready for our second meal. We feasted with our new Iraqi friend until the wee hours, while listening to a local band at a restaurant called Amasi. The band was composed of a singer and traditional acoustic Arab instruments: an *oud* (a fretless lute), a *qanun* (a highly tunable, plucked zither), a violin, a *nay* (an ancient cane flute), and a *dumbek* (drum). We then moved into Ali's apartment and met his younger brother, Haydar.

Streets of Amman: a chilly winter day.

Rising early the next morning, we went to the Iraqi embassy to apply for visas. They were declined. Saddam Hussein's rules dictated that Americans must be invited by an official Iraqi organization before visas could be issued. Later in the day we made phone calls to Baghdad with Ali's help and spoke with members of the Baghdad Musicians' Association, whose names we knew through the Arab musician grapevine. They promised to arrange an official invitation for us.

Ali had been in Baghdad when the bombing occurred during the Gulf War in 1991. "One night I was awakened by a flash and explosion so big and so bright, so much bigger than the rest that I thought: 'that's the nuclear

8

one!' But I just rolled over and went back to sleep. We did enjoy being asked to escort various girls here and there to help them. It made us feel strong and proud. Somehow, when you are in the middle of all the explosions, you have no choice other than to surrender to the situation and do the best you can."

Kristina with our Iraqi refugee friend, Ali. He is part of an extended family whose members now live all over the globe: from Baghdad to Jordan, to Tunisia, to Los Angeles.

Ali moved to Jordan from Baghdad five years ago. Here in Amman he has established himself as a web-page designer, and has considerable computer skills. He is supporting his younger brother and is preparing to welcome his mother and another younger brother into his household. His father died a few years ago; now he is the eldest male family member. This position comes with very clear-cut responsibilities in Arab society.

While running his business, Ali simultaneously offers us his constant, boundless hospitality. "My brother will have to quit being lazy when our mother gets here. She makes us get up early every morning." Ali's brother had opened a small toy store in the neighborhood, but sales were negligible. His true passion was to be a cartoonist. After getting to know us for a few days, he showed us his private world of notebooks filled with sketches.

These cartoons of his could eventually evolve into a new line of super-hero comic strips, but how could this happen? How can he publish his work when he is technically an illegal immigrant in Jordan, and must keep a low profile? We all seemed to know, without putting words to it, that his creativity would not easily find an outlet in his current situation.

Every day we fast, along with the entire population here in Jordan, until about 5 p.m., when the sun sets and it is *iftar* (time to eat again). We stay up late at night. Men walk through the neighborhoods at 4:00 a.m., playing large drums loudly to remind us all to eat the last foods before the sun rises and the next day's fast begins. We are into the last week of the month of fasting and the recorded calls to prayer are being lengthened and augmented by other live prayer 'readers' who stand in the streets and sing. The neighborhoods are filled with the sounds of these calls to prayer, especially at night. Islam is very present. Ali, a Shiite Muslim, has been explaining all the local customs and beliefs about men, women, marriage, and divorce.

Ali calls our musician contacts in Iraq nearly every day. It seems that the letter of invitation has been written and is now being signed and stamped by the appropriate officials. It will be sent to the Iraqi Embassy here in Amman and we will be granted admission to the country. We don't know how long this will take—a few more days, we guess.

During the evenings Ali invites some of his visiting Iraqi relatives over for food and we all, of course, enjoy singing popular songs together. I know at least a dozen such songs well enough to play the melodies on my oud while we sing.

One of Ali's uncles came to dinner with his new bride. They were bubbling with new-found love and cuddliness and it was fun to watch their endless flirting. This uncle had been in the Iraqi army for many years and had fought during the wars with Iran. During those years, Saddam Hussein had been strongly subsidized by the American government, of course, as the Iranian government had been the big enemy. Ali implied that, because of his uncle's military background in Iraq, he might be able to help us get our visas. At some point during the evening we discussed this possibility with him. "Would you be willing to claim to be supporters of Saddam's government?" he asked at one point. "Of course not!" we replied.

Ali's uncle didn't say so, but I got the definite feeling that, without such a declaration, he would not be able to be of much help in getting us into Iraq. In fact, it was after this conversation that Ali began commenting to us that he doubted whether our request for visas would be granted.

Several days passed. We received the news that Ali's mother would be arriving the next day from Baghdad. Kristina and I moved into a small, $9/night hotel in the old city center. While exploring this part of Amman, Kristina, a Palestinian man, and I were interviewed on the streets by a roving BBC reporter. "Who would you side with, Bush or Bin Laden?" she asked. "Well, neither!" we all three responded in turn.

"Were you afraid to come here?" she asked Kristina and me. "No, not at all—we are surrounded by very sweet people here," we replied. "We have come on a musical mission of peace, to make it clear that there are many Americans who believe sharing music is a better option than seizing power by military force."

The Palestinian insisted he had no problem getting along with people anywhere, that it's the leaders who create the problems. "Why is the U.S. government so concerned about Iraq, when Israel is obviously the one with the nuclear weapons?" he asked. "The only country in the world to ever actually use nuclear weaponry was the U.S."

While walking in the center of the old marketplace, a part of Amman filled with crowded streets and tiny shops placed in endless labyrinthine alleyways, we wander into a little music shop. There are lots of ouds hanging in the window; I ask for one and sit down. I play a little and then the shop owner, Jihad, plays, too. He gives me some suggestions about my right hand technique. Little by little, we sing songs from Syria, Iraq, Egypt, Lebanon, and Greece. Tea is ordered and we all settle in to get to know each other. Another man with a bright, beaming energy in his face arrives and sits down to begin a chess game. After the game, and at our insistence, he picks up a violin. Everybody in the shop—there are five or six of us—is saying this man is a professional. The violinist says he also writes children's songs. He then plays Yam Saharni, an Um Kolthoum piece. Very passionate playing!

Jihad's Music Shop: a place for musicians to congregate. Here we exchange knowledge of scales and techniques and find out who is currently playing in town.

Everyone sings along during the vocal parts.

Kristina and I share that we are hoping to get our visas to enter Iraq so that America can be known to have sent something musical. "Yes, yes! Very wonderful!" they all cheer. "The Iraqis are wonderful people! They will treat you very nicely!"

We are getting hundreds of loving and supportive e-mails from America, and enjoy the feedback and sense of being in contact.

We pass another music store with ouds hanging in the window. Inside, we find a Turk born in northern Iraq, and a Palestinian woman born in Haifa, an Arab city on the Mediterranean coast. Haifa is north of Tel Aviv, the capitol of Israel. I play an Um Kolthoum piece from Egypt and they both sing along with Kristina. The woman has fairly good English skills and shows us pictures of her two sons and four daughters, who all "sing very well. One of my sons plays the oud like his father did." She shows us a picture of her now-deceased husband playing the oud.

"We had to leave our house in Haifa in 1947, when the Israeli soldiers asked us to leave," she explained. "I was just a child. We left everything—the furniture, all our possessions. We thought we would only be gone for a short time. We lived in Nablus for three years, but there was not much work so we came here to Amman. Eventually we could afford to have a house. I went back to Haifa once to see our family's house. The Jewish people living in it let me look inside. They had subdivided it into four parts: two apartments each with two stories. We had had high ceilings so they added another floor halfway up. I don't know when we will finally get our house back. It's very beautiful there, close to the sea." I have noticed that none of the maps here in Jordan show anything called 'Israel' in what is labeled 'Palestine.'

The Turkish man plays *Never on Sunday* on the oud, and I sing along in Greek. He then plays a song from Turkey called *Ushkadara gider iken*. I sing some of the Turkish words along with him.

We tell them that we are hoping to go into Iraq. "Wonderful. Yes, a good thing to do. They will treat you very well. And maybe you can find an Iraqi oud!" The Palestinian woman seemed to know that very fine ouds are made in Iraq.

Ali has come down with the flu. He sounds very miserable now when we talk with him over the phone. He is worried that we are no longer sharing his apartment with him, but it is also good for us to be back out on the streets everyday exploring these musical moments. We are very happy that his mother and youngest brother have arrived safely from Baghdad. It was never certain that Ali's 16-year-old brother would be able to get across the border into Jordan. Saddam Hussein did not want young men to leave Iraq; they were valuable to him as potential soldiers.

It is Saturday, December 12th, 2002. The calls to prayer are sounding in the background now. I think tomorrow is the end of the Ramadan feast, *Aid al Fitr*. The daytime fasting will then come to an end and a three-day celebration will begin.

On the last night of Ramadan the streets fill with shoppers. Thousands throng the shops until past midnight as they prepare for a round of family gift-giving reminiscent of our Christmas.

Kristina and I sit on the ancient stone steps of the Roman Theater here in the heart of old town Amman, while red, blue and green doves circle endlessly overhead,. The doves have been painted or dyed under their wings by their owners. They fly in circles around the houses where they were raised from chickhood. Ali, doesn't have a great opinion of the bird owners. "I don't think it is fair to train these doves to feel like they are only able to fly around one house."

Playing with Children in downtown Amman. The little girl on my left has been quietly slipping me sunflower seeds from her pockets in between songs.

Once again we play a song of Um Kolthoum, the Egyptian musical super-goddess of the Arab world. Children are playing all around the theater, climbing the steep stairs, laughing and yelling while parents and older brothers or sisters watch. We smile at the children as we sing and they gather around. They smile back with their eyes and their faces. A little six-year-old girl snuggles up behind me and offers me sunflower seeds.

We sing another song, an Iraqi song this time. The children are gathering in a tighter and tighter group around us. Soon the crowd is at least one hundred strong. They clap and sing along, and when we finish a song, they cheer. Some of the older folks begin to approach and sing with us, too.

Suddenly a young boy grabs my hand on the oud and prevents me from continuing! The call to prayer has begun in the background from a nearby mosque. We wait until it is completed, then begin another Egyptian song. The people all know this one and sing along. I reach the end of the song and begin a *mawal* (improvisational singing which follows certain traditional patterns) in *maqam rast,* one of many exotic Arabic musical scales. The crowd screams with delight, and I realize that I am expressing something deeply Arab with my singing.

Downtown Amman in the old Roman Theater: the crowd of friendly children grows as we sing song after song. Always polite, direct and well-behaved, these children make us feel very welcome.

"Come down into the center of the theater so there is more room," suggest some. "No, this is fine—stay here!" insist others. "Where are you from?" we are asked. "America," we reply. "Very good—welcome!"

The doves are still circling in the afternoon sunlight, glowing in their brilliant painted colors. The pigeon owners have taken the young doves and cut their wing feathers just enough so they can't fly too far. They become accustomed to flying just short distances. The owners then let the feathers grow back, and the doves can fly all day, but now they have been trained to fly only around the owner's house. At night they are taken inside and painted in brilliant colors. Whether this is good or bad, I don't know. It certainly is different from what we do with our 'doves', or pigeons, as we call them in Colorado.

After a few more songs we agree to meet again the next day, *insha'Allah* (God willing). We begin to move toward the exit of the Roman Theater. A policeman approaches and says that it might be dangerous for the small kids to create such a large crowd. "But," he says, "you are welcome to play your oud and sing here whenever you want to." It is clear that he has also been enjoying the singing and is only dutifully expressing a note of caution because of the steepness of the stone stairs inside the theater. Groups of children gather for Kristina to photograph them. The camera doesn't want to function. Stupid camera. Only half of the time you push the button does it take a picture.

After a sip of Turkish coffee, a bit of hummus, tomato-cucumber salad, some chicken and a bit of baklava, we dropped in at Jihad's music store again. We hung out and sang an Um Kolthoum piece and a Fairuz piece, and traded in my cheap travel oud for a nicer Iraqi one, which had been made in Baghdad.

Later in the evening we wander into a part of town which has nice hotels and fancy taxis. We ask, "Where are the music clubs with older styles of Arabic music?" We approach two different cab drivers with this question, only to find ourselves being guided into restaurants featuring modern keyboard-based bands. The music is too loud; we don't stay long. We return to Amasi and enjoy more of the artful, older music.

Our Arabic books and song lyric sheets are our constant companions, and every day we plough through new material. Kristina is fascinated for the moment with learning the writing system, while I am finding that my conversations with the taxi drivers can frequently remain at least half in Arabic, especially if we stick to simple subjects like "turn left at the next corner, please."

Lisa and Kristina: Lisa has just returned from Nablus, on the Palestinian West Bank, where she lived and worked to try and procure basic freedoms for Palestinan people. Upon returning home to Wales, she will work to educate British citizens about the Palestinian reality.

After the three-day *Aid al Fitr* holiday, which follows Ramadan, we begin checking again to see if we're any closer to being issued Iraqi visas, but it's not so easy right now for us Americans to get into Iraq. Honestly, I feel that our function as musical missionaries of peace from America to the Arab world is being carried out just as well here in Jordan as it would be in Iraq, but because the attention of the whole world is on Iraq right now, it seems we should carry our mission there if we can.

If we were a group of at least five Americans, we could be issued visas and shepherded as a 'tourist group' by Iraqi 'minders,' or government guides. We would be given very limited freedom in such a situation. It would be much better to be issued our visas as musicians invited to perform by the Iraqi Musicians' Association. We would then, hopefully, have more freedom inside Baghdad, if we were to ever get there. We heard from a young Welsh friend, Lisa, whom we met here in Amman, that a friend of hers has been waiting two months for his Iraqi visa!

Lisa just finished living in the Palestinian West Bank as part of an international solidarity group who go in and try and help Palestinians. After three months in Nablus she is returning to Britain to try to educate people about the situation.

She lived with various Palestinian families. She would walk out with the school children to show solidarity in breaking the curfew which prohibited Palestinian schoolchildren from going to school. The Palestinian parents believe their children must become educated, and refuse to abide by the curfew. Lisa walked out with them in front of the tanks. She received curses from some of the Jewish settlers.

We asked her what it was like being a young blonde-haired woman alone in Palestine. She said that she was proposed to over and over again, politely, of course. She learned something one day, she said, watching a very beautiful young Palestinian woman who was being admired by the young men. Instead of feeling uncomfortable or threatened, the young woman wiggled a little bit to show that she appreciated the admiration. Suddenly, Lisa said, she realized that acknowledging the attraction was easier than trying to resist it. She said she never felt threatened. Her impression is that women are much safer alone here than they are in many parts of the Western world.

Tonight Baghdad came to us. Ali's mother had requested to hear our Arabic singing, so we were able to provide a songfest for them during the evening. Iraqis in Baghdad are, of course, feeling quite nervous these days. Kristina and I may be "on our way to Baghdad" for some time to come. It's impossible to predict, so it feels good when we perform for the local Iraqi community here in Amman.

Around noon we sat in a downtown Amman park. I began to play the oud. Soon a few passersby paused and listened. After another few minutes, people gathered and began to smile. Another few minutes, and some began to sing along and clap and dance. We are the mysterious, but welcome, strangers from America who sing in Arabic. Sometimes people can't help laughing at our funny pronunciation, but they love to sing along with us.

An hour of music passes. We take a few photos; families and various individuals want to have their pictures taken with their arms draped over the American oud player's shoulders.

Singing in Amman

Later we get the film developed. We drop by a smoky coffee shop, drink some tea and pass the photos around to some men playing backgammon. They all smile. A one-eyed man with a horrendous scar reaching more than halfway around his neck and across his face comes and sits down beside me and extends his hand. "Are you Muslim?" he can't resist asking. He seems slightly surprised when I tell him I am not. He enjoys looking at our freshly developed photographs with us.

It's time to get our Jordanian visas renewed. We wait at the local police station for the four policemen on duty to get finished singing their favorite popular song and, after several minutes of listening to their songs finally make our request. "Of course! Come right in!" we are told by the smiling officers. This is a music-loving society on all levels, it seems.

Groups of kids and adults in a park in Downtown Amman happy to sing along.

We make another late-night visit to our favorite live music venue, Amasi. We are heartily greeted. At the table next to us we see a family of four: a dad, mom, son and a young daughter who dances beautifully and sensually, as Arab Middle Easterners do.

We take a taxi back to the center of the city. Nearly every night we walk the streets of this city, frequently until 4:00 a.m., and feel very safe. A few sleepy policemen are on post, but nothing ever seems to require their attention. No guards are required near the public ATMs, nor at the numerous Gold Market jewelry stores.

The taxi driver listed all major world heads of government for me last night and divided them all into 'good' or 'bad'. News comes in many forms here in Amman, and history is told from ten thousand different perspectives. Remember, whatever you think is TRUE is, at best, only true, and could quite possibly be either false or FALSE.

A park in Amman: each child in this family comes to say hello to Kristina.

Always, always, always—we must return to the music. Verbal realities are only doorways into confusion and conflict. We must return to the beauty of the children's faces; the mothers' faces; the fathers' faces.

This evening we visited a monkey in a cage in a local pet shop. He had very human-looking eyes and a low, non-verbal, grunting voice. "See you later," we told him. There are many cats living in the streets of Amman, but no dogs.

Every spare moment now, Kristina is diving into learning the Arabic writing system to help her with remembering words and phrases. She either has her books open or we are quizzing the waiter on how to pronounce something. Kristina enjoys wandering the city by herself, now that we have a basic feel for the geography.

As for me, every day my mind hungrily scans the dictionaries and the grammar books, familiarizing itself with new words and phrases, faster than I can find ways to try them out. And every day my mind scans its inner recesses: "What was that word, anyway?" Crunch! My mind is trying too hard, trying to work too fast! Where did that habit come from? Talking and being with Kristina helps me move at a smoother pace. My mind works a lot better when it's not frantic with eagerness.

We spent a day with Ali, his mother, Suaad, and his two younger brothers. Suaad, who cooked dinner for us, told us more about the effects of the 1991 Gulf War. People who were exposed to the bombing in Baghdad break out in painful skin rashes. Little scratches that would have been nothing become ulcerated sores. The babies born are frequently horrendously deformed. Suaad has had these rashes and sores on her own body.

These are the survivors of a once well-to-do Iraqi family now reduced, through no fault of their own, to poverty, unstable health and uncertain futures as refugees: Iraqi refugees joining the vast crowd of Palestinians now making the best of it in Amman. Jordan is a country which many Middle East analysts have defined as being built on the disasters of war in the Middle East. Palestinian refugees displaced by the ongoing Israeli occupation account for upwards of 70% of Jordan's population, while it is estimated that upwards of 500,000 Iraqi refugees have fled the U.S. occupation of Iraq into Jordan (as of December, 2005, the time of publishing this 2nd edition).

Kristina's new dress:
a gift from Suaad.

Suaad told stories for hours about the lives of her brothers and sisters, who are now scattered all over the globe. Kristina burst into tears at some point. Ali maintains optimism and hope, however, that he, the eldest son and now the sole bread-winner for the family, can earn enough to rebuild a home someday. He doesn't yet know where.

Ali's mother took Kristina by the hand and persuaded her to try on a beautifully embroidered dress. She then insisted it was a gift. "When an Arab family persuades you to just 'try something on,' don't think it's not a gift," said Ali.

This morning, just as I left the hotel, I was invited to share tea with a Palestinian shopkeeper who runs a little repair workshop. I sang him a piece of Abd 'al Halim's *Sawah* and he grabbed me and planted kisses all over my face.

Kristina and Suaad, mother of Ali. She has just arrived safely out of Baghdad. Her Iraqi house was subsequently destroyed in the bombing.

We are getting to know the musicians who play late at night at Amasi: Bassam on oud, Sa'ad on percussion, Sabah on violin. Bassam let me play his oud again after their performance last night.

It has been raining for three or four days now. This is very good for crops growing in the fields, but it has temporarily put a stop to our street concerts.

Aqaba and Southern Jordan

Kristina and I got on a bus and rode south for four hours, traveling beside the Dead Sea until we arrived in the port city of Aqaba. We wandered through the spice and meat market, beside the Red Sea. Some boys pointed at my oud case and cleaned off some metal stairs for us to sit down. With racks full of skinned goats hanging in the background, we sang three or four songs for the enthusiastic, all-aged crowd. Kristina pointed at my watch to remind me that it was almost time for the afternoon call to prayer. We stopped our songs when we heard it begin.

Our songs led to invitations to have coffee from one of the local butcher-shop owners. We did our best in Arabic and discovered that yes, his grand-father and his father had owned the shop before him. He made motions of sleeping to indicate that they had already passed away. I thought maybe he meant that his dad was taking a nap next door. He repeated the sleeping body language, putting his two hands beside his cheek but this time adding a throat slicing motion to indicate that what he meant was that they had died. There were pictures of his grandfather and father on the wall. We climbed up to his office and took some photos of us in various combinations. Kristina declined sitting on his lap. We entered the spice shop next door for more tea and felt the delicious aroma of piles of freshly ground spices enter our noses.

We walk down by the edge of the Gulf of Aqaba here on the Red Sea and sit on a low concrete wall. Young men listen to us in the gathering darkness as we sing. Kristina sings Fairuz. We sing again songs of Abd 'al Halim, Farid al Atresh, Um Kolthoum by Mohammad Abd 'al Wahab, Sabah Fakhri. More free tea is brought and offered to us by the young men. It is now dark.

A butchershop in Aqaba: we are invited to sing in the marketplace.

Evening music beside the Red Sea.

Wandering around the town later, I checked out the local big hotel singer and keyboard show—too loud, and it's hard to relate to the people there. Kind of painful on the ears, but fun to watch guys get up and and dance *dabkeh* (Arab line dance) with each other. The singer, a young female with long flowing bleached blond hair, reigned queen. The boys in the crowd got up when she beckoned them and clapped when she clapped. But the music was too loud for me. I couldn't stay.

Next morning. Breakfast. Arabic coffee. Yum. A Bedouin guy approaches, asking about my oud. We play him songs at the coffee shop, then go down beside the Red Sea and sing him another song. "Okay," he announces, "you are now part of my family. I want to take you to meet my uncle near Wadi Rum, up in the desert. He plays oud very good. You not tourists. No charge. Just you pay for gas for the camel. My name is Jafar."

We climb into his 'camel,' a vintage Datsun Patrol, which is held together with the Bedouin version of duct tape and baling wire. We stop for tea with Jafar's cousin, who is a watchman for a local highway construction project. Kristina likes his cute puppies. Dogs are definitely a rarity in the Arab world. They are found only outside the cities in the rural areas, where they can be used for hunting. Jafar says his cousin doesn't really have to watch anything in order to fulfill his "watchman" job, so he has time to hang out and play with his dogs.

Jafar, our new Bedouin friend. We discover the
honor of being adopted into his family.

27

An hour or two north we enter Al Quwayra, a Bedouin town. "My uncle lives in that house," points Jafar. "And my other uncle lives in that house. And another uncle in that house—another in that house. Actually, I have twenty uncles who live here!"

Jafar's 'camel.' We are off into the desert on a Bedouin road with musical family members.

We putt and sputter, the 'camel' grinding its gears; the slave cylinder, which operates the clutch, is no longer functioning. We stop at another cousin's house, go upstairs, meet his cousin, wife, and children. We have tea and play the oud. This cousin, Hussein, plays oud very well and in many styles. His eyes shine brightly into mine as he plays several songs. I play several songs back to him. Jafar is very happy with the situation. We all get in the 'camel': Jafar, Hussein, his wife Zeinab, their six-month-old daughter Taif, and four- and six-year-old sons Sa'ad and Aktam, Kristina and me. We take many blankets and stop to buy chicken.

We drive off in 4-wheel-drive through the sand on a Bedouin road into high, arid desert. We stop at a natural stone bridge and climb up through the rocks. Hussein is a spider on the rocks. He zooms away up into the cliffs.

Kristina and I take Taif, Zeinab, their two sons, and my oud and climb up into the eye of the stone arch. We sing Lebanese *dabkeh* (dance) music. Zeinab knows the words and sings along. Jafar takes our picture from down below. The sun is approaching the horizon.

We sputter off across the desert, stopping every little while to refill and bleed the clutch master cylinder. When the engine stops, it can only be restarted by connecting the terminals on the starter motor with a wrench under the hood.

A 'Bedouin Road' leads us for miles into the labyrinth of sand and rock formations.

We pull into a small side canyon of one of the many tall, wind-carved, sandstone mountains and empty out the Datsun. We gather dry brush for firewood, make two fires, spread blankets, cook chicken, and make tea. Hussein removes his shoes, washes his feet, and beautifully sings the call to prayer. It echoes inside the canyon walls. We watch stars appear. The temperature drops into the low 40's. We add more twigs to the fire and play songs on the oud and nay. For many more hours we are treated to a feast of Bedouin music and poetry. Finally we curl up under the blankets under the stars to find sleep—or let sleep find us.. I hear everyone breathing and snoring around me, but I don't fall asleep. I watch the moon move from 12 o'clock to 3 o'clock across the heavens.

Natural Stone Bridge in Southern Jordan

Singing Lebanese Dance Music with Zeinab and children.

-- Natural Bridge Viewed from Other Side --

The stars witness your sleeplessness
as you dream of your loved ones.

Hussein taught me this poem in Arabic and I felt a little piece of Arabic soul glide into my body.

A Small Side Canyon: a favorite place to make camp and spend the night.

Jafar and Zeinab in our Bedouin camp.

Kristina and Hussein, a marvelous musician.

Jafar is a very strong and efficient 25-year-old, apparently wise way beyond his years. He expounds on the art of balancing work and life: "Not so much work that you lose yourself and forget who you are. We value the silence of this desert."

Morning comes. Jafar is first up, with fire and tea for all of us. Hussein plays more songs on the oud: Bedouin, Kaliji, Omani and Yemeni styles. Each has its own rhythmic pattern of picking. We go for a two-hour hike and Hussein climbs way up to the tops of two mountains while we climb on the lower parts. Back at the camp, we attempt to start the Datsun. After fifteen minutes of pumping and engine cranking, it sputters into life. We bleed the clutch, pile in the blankets and off we go.

We stop at an ancient cistern, obviously carved by hand out of the rock. "Water is the 'gold' of the desert," Jafar reminds us. I point at the right front tire, which has lost half of its air. "It will be ok," says Jafar. Stopping two or three more times to bleed the clutch brings us to the point of disaster with the tire. It is flat, shredded and halfway off the rim. Still, we drive through the sand.

Stubborn lug nut adds to our host of mechanical nightmares.

Finally reaching a small, paved road not far from the village, we stop, jack up the front end and prepare to put on the spare tire. Stripped lug nuts make this impossible. Hussein and Jafar work furiously for half an hour to no avail. A passing truck stops. We try with the driver's tools, but nothing works.

Hussein and Zeinab reflect the warmth of their love.

Another whole Bedouin family of brothers from the nearby village uses their tractor, with its big wheels, to drag us to the edge of the pavement, hoping, somehow, a miracle will take place. Instead of a miracle we find that the clutch will no longer function and we cannot drive any further on the shredded tire. They tow us into the yard of their house. A low, concrete block wall contains sheep, goats, doves and several decades' worth of discarded fuel cans and tractor parts.

A very elderly bearded grandfather sits on his prayer mat in the sun where two more ancient diesel tractors are receiving patching and love. The grandfather has his shoes parked neatly behind his mat and has obviously already passed into some kind of after-life here on earth, wherein the physical work is done by others. His apparent function now is to pray and to witness.

Hussein: a modern Bedouin. Excellent musician, a lover of Arab poetry and, as we discovered in the desert, an agile rock climber.

A very sturdy man appears with welding equipment from the shed. We are going to torch off the offending lug nut. Eventually, the tire is changed! We all sit down for tea. Myriad flies buzz around us. Discussion turns to the broken clutch. More attention is needed there: more fluid; more bleeding of air in the lines. At last it's back in operation and we're off! Triumphant, we cruise into the yard beside Hussein's house. Zeinab makes hummus, *fuul* (fava beans in olive oil), olives, tomatoes, bread, and potatoes for breakfast. More tea is served, and more songs played.

Finally, we kiss and embrace our Bedouin friends, who never did ask for money. I attempt to give Jafar and Hussein each a few dollars. "No, you are our friends, they say. "But it is just a gift," I insist, and put it in their hands.

We climb into a taxi bound for Wadi Musa. We walk for six hours through the ancient town of Petra, carved 2000 years ago out of the solid, living red and purple sandstone cliffs in the bottoms of myriad labyrinthine canyons. It

Petra: a 2000-year-old tribute to the magnificent craftsmanship of the Nabatean tribe. Fear of every-thing 'Middle Eastern' has caused a drop in tourism since 2001, from a rate of a thousand people a day down to forty people a day.

is incredible, but still foremost in my consciousness are the sweet memories of Hussein and his wife's atmosphere of sweet love: I had become addicted to their smiling eyes!

Before the September 11th attack on New York and Washington, Petra was visited by close to one thousand tourists a day. The town of Wadi Musa was growing rapidly to meet the needs of these visitors. Now, they say, they are lucky to see forty tourists a day. Many of the hotels are going out of business.

The small hotel we stayed in was run by an extended family. Every time we returned to our room we were greeted by a different person. Obviously no longer able to pay employees, these different family members took turns running the place. There was plenty of time to visit with them; time seemed to have frozen in place.

We found ourselves to be the lone patrons of restaurants. A young Palestinian waiter we befriended in one such restaurant found himself similarly stopped in his life plans; his bride-to-be, who resides in Gaza, has been waiting for over a year now for him to be able to obtain permission to cross the border and make the traditional, formal request of marriage to her parents. Because of the impossibility of making these border crossings, their wedding plans must remain on hold. The slow wind erosion of the two-thousand-year-old stone palaces in the canyons below is setting the pace of time for the entire region.

We rode the mini-buses back to Aqaba through the town of Ma'an. Army tanks were stationed here and there in Ma'an because of recent trouble: several deaths from fighting with the army. According to the Jordanian Times, some of the folks in Ma'an were revolting because they were angry about the Jordanian government's unwillingness to take a stand against the U.S. regarding upcoming violence against Iraq. The local folks, however, said it's just a local problem resulting from some 'bad people.'

Arriving back in Aqaba, we are immediately spotted and greeted by Jafar. The Datsun 'camel' is in better shape and roadworthy once again. After we get settled in our hotel, we go to his house in the Bedouin suburbs and eat the dinner which he has cooked. He has invited several neighbors over to listen to us play oud and sing some of our Arabic repertoire.

He offers us his house, but we prefer the privacy of the hotel for now. He writes us a poem and gives us a small teapot. We turn down his other offered gift of a piece of feathery, white coral. "How could we carry it in our backpacks all the way back home without breaking it?" we asked.

Everyone focuses on our music as we play in Jafar's home. The more they focus, the better we play and sing. One of the guests also plays the oud very well.

Driving back to our hotel in Jafar's Datsun later that night, he tells us "You know, I have to confess something. When we left for the desert and I asked for you to pay for the cost of the gas only, I put more gas in the tank than I really needed to. I put in 20 JD (Jordanian Dinars), and all we really needed was maybe 15. I was thinking to siphon off the extra five few liters and make 5 JD. I tell you this because I feel badly that, although I told you that you were family and that we would go to the desert without your having to pay anything except expenses, I was still secretly trying to make a little money from you. Now I have told you this truth and I feel better!" Such is the soul of Jafar. I thanked him again for our adventures together, and told him not to worry about it.

Walking once more down the marketplace streets of Aqaba, people remember us and invite us to sit and play oud and sing in their restaurant, but we are tired. "Tomorrow," I tell them. We are now famous here on the streets.

Back in town again, I'm able to get a call through into Baghdad, only to learn our visa applications are still being held up. With only a few days left before our booked flight departs for our return to the U.S., the chances for our Iraqi visa to come through are looking dim. We do, however, have time for a quick trip into the West Bank. Lisa, our new friend from Wales, had been living in Nablus. We decide to head in that direction, and plan to pass through the cities of Jericho and Ramallah.

The West Bank and Ramallah

At the bridge over the river Jordan, on the border of the West Bank, we met a Palestinian family waiting to board the next bus. We sang a few bars of familiar, popular songs. Seeing the little bag of Lay's potato chips I was holding for my pre-breakfast snack, they said, "Now we are very careful not to buy anything from America. Nothing, nothing, nothing American! See our two-year-old boy? He's only two and he already says he wants to die shooting Israeli soldiers in Jerusalem! Look at what is becoming of our children!" We then sang some more Arabic songs. Big smiles broke out.

A special bus which only crosses the bridge finally arrives. We cross and wait for another passport check. The atmosphere is tense. The prices for the taxis are ten times higher than they were in Jordan. The driver tells us we cannot pass through downtown *Ariha* (Jericho in Arabic), which is currently closed by the Israeli soldiers. We would have to cross too many checkpoints and change from one car to another at each barricade. We ride over tiny backroads away from Jericho, toward Ramallah. Palestinian drivers know the routes with the least number of Israeli checkpoints and use those roads, even though they are nothing more than dirt tracks through the canyons. At times we stop and wait. The roads are too narrow to allow two-way traffic.

I am playing the oud and singing from the back seat of our taxi; Kristina leans over and sings with the driver in the front seat. Another taxi filled with Palestinians cheers our music from across the road where we stop and wait. We are quiet later as we wait to pass through two checkpoints near the outskirts of Ramallah. The taxis are not allowed to actually go into Ramallah, we must go on foot. We walk through a labyrinth of concrete barriers past Israeli bunkers and coils of razor wire. The Israeli soldiers ask us what we want to do there. "Just tourists—we are musicians," we tell them. They look at us coldly but, with our American passports, we are allowed to pass.

We walk into the city. It's further than we think, and eventually we take another taxi to the city center. It's 4 or 5 p.m. and we are ready for 'breakfast'. We enter a place that advertises 'Mexican Food'. This is a rarity! The "tacos" taste distinctly Middle Eastern, but still spicy and good. We find a hotel and bargain with the manager. We sing a few phrases of an Abd 'al Halim song. Big smiles.

Taysir and his wife in their restaurant in Ramallah celebrate a wedding anniversary and invite us to sing.

Following our noses and various pieces of advice on the street, we enter Mataam Ziryab, a coffee shop, art gallery and restaurant, oud in hand. It is around 9:00 p.m. The Palestinian owner, Taysir Barakat, is sitting down with his wife to celebrate their 14th wedding anniversary. He is a successful international artist. The walls are covered with his latest work: paintings created by burning images onto wooden plaques. We get to know the owners for a couple of hours.

Taysir and Kristina Dance late into the evening in Ramallah.

Taysir's wife tells us of the latest curfews and closings. Only a month or so ago, the town was cut off from electricity and phone service.

A few weeks ago, Israeli soldiers surrounded their house because they thought a toy gun her 10-year-old son was playing with might be real. They had been watching him play through binoculars from the settlement above the Barakats' house. The soldiers threatened to destroy the house with bulldozers if it was not found. Finally the boy, shaking and sobbing, was able to lead the soldiers to some alley where he had already thrown the toy gun away. "If you ever buy another one, we will kill you and your family," he was told by one of the soldiers. He is still shaken from this experience and having nightmares.

Our new friend Taysir, the owner of Mataam Ziryab, tells us that just the day before he had met with Jane Fonda. She had just returned to the West Bank in an expression of solidarity with the Palestinian people. "It was an artist-to-artist meeting," he explains.

*Singing with Palestinians
in Taysir's restaurant in Ramallah*

*Palestinians in a Ramallah hotel use a TV remote
as a pretend microphone while we sing.*

He gives us three prints of some of his earlier works and talks about the dream states he enters in order to create. I read the poetry he has written about his inspiration to paint a series of watercolors. The series is about the exodus of Arabs from Granada, Spain, back in 1492. I am impressed with the translation of his poetry. He brings a quality of thick dream mist into his work. "And in this restaurant, I use all kinds of scraps and recycled materials to decorate the interior, " he explains. "And I made the light fixtures from old paper," adds his wife.

"We exhibit the artwork of many different people here and we want people to be able to sit and be comfortable, drink a coffee, and be surrounded by the art. It's different from walking through a museum-like gallery."

They are raising their three children here in Ramallah in spite of the difficulties. I wonder how he maintains his artistic focus in the face of the heavy distraction of being under varying degrees of siege.

Invited to perform, we bring out the oud and sing. A group of young women encourage us; they sing along and ask for more. Kristina locks heart to heart with one of the young women. They sing expressively together as the waiters listen in the background. We realize we have good new friends in Ramallah. They tell us to visit again.

Walking through the streets we notice a Christmas tree in a shop window. We must be in a Christian part of town. Moments later a car zooms by us with Santa Claus, dressed in his bright red suit, leaning out the window ringing a Christmas bell!

We return to the hotel past midnight to find a group of Palestinian men sitting downstairs in the lobby. They ask me to bring out the oud. Soon we are busy with song again. One of the desk clerks uses the TV remote for a pretend microphone. It's late at night, and quiet except for our singing. We focus on the music and they help us with the Arabic lyrics. It gets really good. We sing and laugh and smile. Sometime in the wee hours we go upstairs to bed.

Rising early at 9:00 a.m., we leave the hotel and take a cab to see the remains of the government buildings in which Yasser Arafat is under seige. Only the central building is intact. It is surrounded by the rubble and twisted metal of several city blocks of what, we are told, were once government offices.

*Destruction in Yasser Arafat's
Government Headquarters*

*Yasser Arafat was living in the light-colored
building on the far left: the only remaining
structure in the government compound.*

44

The remains of many smashed automobiles which were pulverized under the treads of the tanks are barely recognizable.

We take a taxi back to the checkpoint at the entrance to Ramallah; our packs and oud case are opened and searched. The two Palestinians in line in front of us are denied passage for some reason and are turned back. We ride in a large 'service taxi' back toward Jericho and are held up behind a truck hauling a huge Israeli tank. Above us on various hilltops we see what look like Israeli settlements. We ask the taxi driver what they are. *"Kibutzes,"* he replies. Confusion and expensive taxi rides follow as we are guided and misguided through various checkpoints and bus stations back to the bridge. We pay a large exit fee to the Israelis at the border and breathe more freely once back on the Jordanian side.

Back in Amman it is cold and raining, but we can come and go as we please, which is a nice freedom. I wonder if those large buses filled with Palestinians we passed near the bridge are still waiting to be allowed to move. Time and time again we are told by Palestinians, "Yes, I have family on the other side of the border, but now it is very difficult for us to get in or out."

We stop by one of our favorite restaurants and order a nice meal. The elderly gentleman who runs the place tells us a secret about his parakeets, which we can see in their cage: "They have laid a little egg! It is very rare for them to do that. Let's hope for a baby bird!"

We were photographed and interviewed by reporters working for an Arabic language newspaper called *Okaz*. Residents of downtown Amman had told them about our singing with the children and families in the parks.

The moment arrives: it's time to get on the airplane and fly back to Colorado. As the Arab world faded into the distance we found ourselves hungering for that soul-to-soul eye contact which we had come to love.

We found ourselves hoping that, with enough people like ourselves all around the world doing some kind of bridge-building work, the war threats coming from Washington, D.C. would be transformed into less violent alternatives.

Colorado

January, 2003

We arrive back in Boulder, Colorado. We are back in the atmosphere of the U.S. media broadcasts again and we feel the outrage, disappointment and pain of watching the apparently inevitable attack on Iraq.

We offer to show some of our photos, tell some of our stories and play a few Arabic songs to a few friends. We expect ten or fifteen people to attend. Eighty people show up. We realize that people in America are hungry for people-to-people reporting about the Arab world. We know that it will be important for us to return there soon.

We stay in touch by e-mail with our Iraqi friend, Ali, in Amman:

> *E-Mail from Cameron to Ali:*
> *Subject: from Cameron and Kristina*
> *Date: Thu, 13 Feb 2003*
>
> *Ali,*
> *We are very worried and upset with the way our government is headed...*
> *Our local newspaper just did a big article about us which came out today:*
> *I hope your family is safe there in Amman...*
> *Please give them all our big love and especially to you...*
> *Cameron*

E-Mail from Ali:
Subject: Re: from Cameron and Kristina
Date: Fri, 14 Feb 2003

Hi;
Thanks, me and my family send our best wishes to you too.
Special Hi from my Mum to kristina.

Regards, Ali

In mid-March I write to those who follow our adventures by e-mail:

"We will be returning to the Middle East in eight days. We feel called to stay in touch with our brothers and sisters in the Arab world. As our nation wages war we feel called to wage peace and will represent an America that is rarely portrayed on TV screens. We wish to do all that we can to cross the bridges of cultural understanding, creating friendships and connecting with the people of these countries through the power of their beautiful music.

"We are members of a gigantic global voice now. We the People insist upon our rights to trade and build and worship and sing and dance on this beautiful green jewel of a planet. We have always felt our psychic connection and now our internet connections are giving us voices and votes which can be counted and we come from every corner of the earth and we say to the old hierarchical governments: "Leave us alone! We have lives to lead! Get out of our way! We are the people and we are the singers and the lovers and the cultivators! We will dismantle the treaties of inequality.

"We will learn each others' languages and songs and a global democracy can now emerge. Those who try to keep their power by instilling fear between peoples can no longer succeed. We have sung and danced together in hundreds of tribal manifestations... oh the songs... oh the dances... oh the courtships... we are done with rule by fear!"

48

Cairo, Egypt

Tuesday, March 25, 2003

We arrived at the airport in Cairo at 3:00 a.m., worried. What will we say to the 25 million souls who call Cairo home? American bombs are falling in Baghdad every day now. I tell the taxi dispatcher in the airport that I am feeling very badly because my American government has chosen the path of attack. He looks into my eyes: "Is that the way you really feel?" he asks. "Yes," I respond. "Then that is what shall determine your destiny, my friend!" he tells me with a smile.

Cairo, Egypt: giant city of twenty-five million people.

Soon we were in the cab, slowly meandering toward downtown. We paused in front of a little hotel ($10/night) so we could take turns playing my nay and sing another song with the cab driver in the car.

Streets of Cairo

Come on, people! Let's remember to be our beautiful and juicy selves. Someday the emerging global democracy will gently make obsolete the current fear-based government/protection rackets. We only have so many precious lives to lead. We cannot afford this waste.

We have been bathing in the warm welcome extended to us everywhere we go here. It's so easy; if you just welcome yourself, then the whole world welcomes you.

Climbing up into the hotel we find eight or nine men, a woman and her newborn girl gathered to enjoy each others' company and ours., singing and talking at 4 o'clock in the morning...We're back in the Arab world!

The next day is a full twelve hours on the streets—bazaars, the Nile, music shops, exotic essential oils and aphrodisiacs, a restaurant with *qanun* (an Arabic zither) and *riq* (tambourine) players, and customers singing along. I experience myself as one of the first of an army of American wanderers who have already lost—lost my heart, that is! We have all surrendered our hearts to the most famous Egyptian Goddess-singer, Um Kolthoum, and now we wander through the alleyways of Cairo. Eternal children of the world, we become the singers when we hear the song.

> *We become the acrobats when we see the dancing,*
> *We become the vendors when we see the selling,*
> *We become the cooks when we taste the cooking.*

The Cairo Bread Truck: this is how your pita bread arrives to your favorite restaurant. Acrobatic skills like this abound in everyday Egyptian life. Car in the way? No problem: a few men can pick it up and move it.

It only took half an hour for my apprehension over being an American to dissolve into this warm bath of Egyptian hospitality.

E-Mail from Ali:
Subject: Re: from cameron and kristina
Date: Sun, 23 Mar 2003

Hi cameron and kristina;

I think of my duty is to do this, I know that you have a big list of people who is against the war in Iraq, but I don't know how much of these people know what really is happening now in Iraq, for the last 2-3 days Basrah south of Iraq is been bombed in a very heavy way, the US Army say they want to shock these people and make them surrender, well, for the only 2 last days there has been about 77 casualties (not talking about the other states of Iraq, like bombing 55 sleeping people at the north of Iraq), one family 5 members I think has been bombed, all dead, I'm attaching the photo of their kid (that is after he died, very shocking), now I can send more and more of these photos, but since the dead people should be respected and not be shown like this I couldn't, specially that it's very painful to watch.
I would be thankful if you forward this as I heard that CNN and other TVs do not show this.

Regards, Ali

We made a dozen new friends on the streets and in the marketplace. All that is necessary is to say "yes!" We weave through endless mazes of people, carts and cars: a human soup as thick as the richest stew. Confidence in the human heart reflects on all sides through this, one of the densest and tightest expressions of human faith on Planet Earth: Cairo.

We tell them that thousands of our American friends back home are sending their greetings through our hearts and songs. Late last night we played oud together in the music shops on Mohammed Ali Street. We tell our new friends that hundreds of our American friends are contributing to support our ability to be here. We tell them that dozens of our Arab-speaking friends back in America are helping us dive more deeply into the songs, language and meaning of the beautiful, ancient cultures of the Arab world.

So there is no doubt, you see:

There is no hesitation about the opening of all of our hearts...
The eyes, as always, speak the truth... There is no fear...
We are truly blessed to be here...
And yes, every moment the war is hurting our hearts...

Still a woman in front of her news-stand on the street corner claps her hands in time to the music from a radio. She is happy about something. A grandmother hobbles through the traffic on bent legs, wincing from the pain, but she is still a part of this celebration of buying and selling, coming and going, talking and listening and feeling, never stopping. Cairo.

Whenever you are ready, come and join this vast human celebration! Forget fear and join us here where the ancient wisdom speaks so clearly.

A rich person is not he who *has the most,*
but rather he who *needs the least...*

We held our own 'demonstration' in Tahrir Square. At the heart of downtown Cairo, it is the same square which was used by thousands of Egyptians to protest the war being waged by America, the 'last surviving superpower'.

We did not hold an 'anti-war demonstration', but rather a 'peace and music demonstration'. We didn't have to explain it, really.

The Egyptians were immediately thrilled to hear us singing their music, and we were surrounded by dozens of smiling, dancing, clapping young men and women. Kristina danced with the young Egyptians, and a three-year-old boy danced exuberantly in the center of the crowd. An old woman with missing teeth pleaded for another verse of a song by Abd al Halim.

At this very same moment, not too far to the east, people are dying in Baghdad. Someone mentions the Iraqi people, and we see tears running down one young Egyptian man's cheeks.

Tahrir Square, Central Cairo. Crowds of young people join us for dance and song. Cameron's face is visible in the center. Bombs are falling in Baghdad at this very moment. Tears flow down these Egyptians' cheeks when they think about this.

For the last few days we have been learning a musical prayer in Arabic, titled *t'ala al batru alaina* (the full moon is rising). We sing this with reverence for the culture in which this tragedy is unfolding. The great Egyptian composer Riyad al Soumbati incorporated this song into an incredible piece he wrote for Um Kolthoum.

Our peace and music demonstration continues. The crowd trades songs with us, many songs we know and don't know, rhythmic chants and beautiful love songs. The oud is passed from person to person. A journalist from an Arab-language newspaper approaches and asks our opinions. Translation happens haltingly.

Central Cairo: we sing and we dance. The girls are enjoying their lollipops.

Now that we have some time and can play on the streets, in the restaurants and schools, we are gradually becoming known around our little downtown Cairo neighborhood.

E-mail from Ali:
Subject: Re: from cameron and kristina
Date: Tue, 25 Mar 2003

Hi;
You asked for more images, well, I'm attaching some, but so far there has been more and more casualties. Last time I heard, Baghdad alone has more than 300 casualties (I'm talk-ing about people). Yesterday, a house that has nothing near it (I mean only houses near it), was hit, and all the family was killed and some neighbors I guess.
The main thing now is Basrah is having some really serious

problems. Since they did not receive the troops with flowers and blessings as Mr. Bush and Blair wanted, they hit the electricity and water supply to it. These people have no water for three days now, and they are using water out of the river and it will cause sickness (massively). This is not all. Today a spokesman of the invading troops has said something that "we will intensify the bombing to break Basrah because it now represents a challenge."

The strange thing is that the UN too is now taking a part in this war. They stopped the supplies of the oil for food, and US and Britain have confiscated Iraqi Money! This started to remind me of bank robbery movies: ok let's hit Iraq and take their money and oil, and blame Iraq for having mass destruction weapons that we used twice on Japan!
Anyway, let's concentrate on Basrah and Nasseriah. (I know these people: they don't like anyone to interfere with them and now they are united as army and people having a skirmish battle to defend their state). Actually it's getting more attention and so there is more bombing now and the local people think it's as a revenge for an Iraqi Farmer taking down an Apache Helicopter with an old rifle that came back from WWI.

The main Idea is that American people should know that this is going somewhere they won't like. It's getting personal. I mean people all over Arab world (ordinary People) are blaming the US and that would not be good. It may mean stuff worse than 9/11. Take it this way: if Iraqis are killed to remove Saddam (which they think is really to invade Iraq and take the oil too), then American people can be hit to get revenge or remove the danger coming from the US, and if the US can stick their noses in Arab stuff then we should stick ours in theirs too.

Anyway, I don't want and pray that it doesn't mean something like WWIII, but it's time for the US people to check if they really have any effect on their country's actions. Or is everything coming only from a few people from Oil companies?

I hope I don't get misunderstood, because as you know I still have American friends and business with them. It's out of my concern for Iraqi safety and peace between Iraqis and Americans that I say these things.   Regards, Ali

This afternoon, thanks to our precious musical connections of friendship, Kristina and I spent several hours playing with teachers at the Cairo College of Music, on Zamalek, an island in the Nile. These music professors say that it is always the same: the people and the governments belong to different species. We, the people, watch helplessly while the governments wreak destruction. We choose to play another classical piece of music with them. We have a qanun, nay, oud and, of course, our voices.

Really, I feel sick inside.

"Come to My House!"

Tonight the men who know us from the hotel invited us to sing and play in the tavern on the corner in our little downtown Cairo neighborhood. Our songs were highly appreciated and we were rewarded with many more bottles of beer than we could possibly drink. Alcohol is not generally consumed in the Islamic world. This place was an exception because we were

The Tavern on the corner: the man holding up his hand had lived for years in Tennessee until recently when, after 9/11, his barn was burned down.

in a slightly upper-class tourist-oriented neighborhood. I felt a bit nervous that, if we stayed late in this place, we might be in over our heads trying to keep up with heated political discussion.

"America is 10,000 miles away," mused one man, showing some anger. "Why are they coming all the way over here to kill our women and babies? No one in Iraq has attacked them...!" He told Kristina that she must write a letter to Laura Bush about this.

Really, I must just hope now that the war ends quickly so that fewer human souls are maimed and killed. But tonight I am reading things on the internet news about the number of deaths, making me lose another level of hope. I guess we were all hoping that somehow these so-called 'smart bombs' could miss all human targets, but it is simply not the case.

E-Mail from Ali:
Subject: Re: website to look at
Date: Thu, 27 Mar 2003

Hi;
I hope you are well!
*I don't know if I'm repeating the news to you. Please tell me
if I am. The statistics I last saw were that casualties reached
3000 Civilian persons. This is not counting what I saw today.
As I said before, since Basrah did not surrender, the bombing
with artillery was increased. What I saw on TV, and I don't
know if your TVs show this or not, is a child with his internal
digestion system out of his body and still alive. This was in
Basrah with other people that were hit.*

*Yesterday about 19 civilians were hit. A bomb hit a market in
Baghdad, because they think this market sells mass destruction weapons, I guess. Photos of burned people were shown
in the TV.*

*Today a whole street in Mosul was hit. Over 50 people (fami-
lies) were killed. A Hospital was hit too today. I don't know
the casualties yet.*

*It seems Bush doesn't understand. He thinks that these are
military places, just because people don't agree with him and
are fighting for their country (which any Iraqi would do for
sure, including me). He sent more troops and asked for more
money.*

*The funny thing is that CNN shows a soldier visiting a fam-
ily or giving away a few Mineral Water boxes as if this is the
blessing from God that Iraqis awaited. He is forgetting that
this wouldn't have happened if the attack had not taken place,
OR if we hadn't been subjected to 13 years of sanctions (as
they call them).*

I just heard a US military man now on the TV saying, "well, the Iraqis don't understand: WHY DO THEY PUT THEIR MILITARY EQUIPMENT IN CITIES!?" and something like "OH, THESE PEOPLE DON'T GIVE UP!" GIVE UP? Our country? For Mr. Bush!?

One more thing, the US forces shot down the Web-site where I used to get the images from and, needless to say, they hit the TV station in Iraq, and the phones of Baghdad. This, of course, includes the water station and electricity plant in Basrah. Oh and many Many Bridges! I will check for another source, BUT, I'm depending on you to deliver this info to others in America.

Regards, Ali

In Tahrir Square in downtown Cairo we were welcomed and told we could consider Egypt our home any time we should choose. That is one of the very touching things we have been told. And yes, we are telling the people here that thousands of people in America receive our e-mail messages, and that news of the sweet nature of Arabic-speaking people is being spread to American homes.

One of the men whom we met tonight in the corner tavern had a farm back in Tennessee. He lived in America for 25 years, raising horses and trying to raise frankincense. After 9/11 his barn was set on fire by local teenagers. Broken-hearted he returned to Egypt. Will he ever go back? He shakes his head.

E-Mail from Ali:
Subject: Re: website to look at
Date: Fri, 28 Mar 2003

Hi;

Just now 52 were killed and many injured in a market bomb-
ing in Baghdad. It was the shua'alah market which is one of
the poorest places and NO WAY is there something military
to target near this market.

Poor Iraqis. It seems Saddam is not enough. Now Bush is
killing them too. I'm sorry to say this, but in my opinion
every American is part of this. Doesn't Bush represent the
United States people? This is not my opinion only. It almost
everybody's I know. Don't get me wrong, but soldiers are
Americans too, right?

Regards, Ali

Although these tragedies seemed like something awful that could *possibly* happen, we chose to hold out hope that somehow they could be avoided. Well, now the unthinkable horrors of war are a living, breathing reality, staring us in the face. What are we to make of the decision-makers who led so many innocent people into this place? What are we to make of those who go to work every day and design these vicious weapons which are now being unleashed on Iraq? Do they think about what they are really doing? We really must make our feelings known. How can we not?

America, as the last surviving superpower, has every opportunity to set an enlightened example of leadership. But America is deploying her own weapons of mass destruction. Who is responsible for losing and wasting that opportunity?

Empires who choose to rule with an iron fist: their days become numbered. Please, Americans, wake up! The flesh on one body is not worth more or less than the flesh on another.

It feels, from close-up here in the Egyptian and Jordanian Arab world, like we are in a whirlwind of a million changing thoughts and emotions. The Arab world is shocked that Iraqis would actually welcome the Americans and surrender so easily. Thank God the bombing is winding down and the lives of young American men and women, as well as the lives of the Iraqi civilians and 'soldiers' (all-to-obviously just people, too) will no longer be in such danger.

Everyone has been wrong and everyone has been right. No matter which 'opinion' we have been holding, pages are turning and the emotionally charged logics are becoming obsolete.

Returning to Aqaba, Jordan, we once again dissolve into groups of friendly locals eager to sing, dance and share tea.

Back to Aqaba, Jordan

Friday, April 11, 2003

Leaving Cairo, we cross the Sinai desert on a bus and proceed north to Jordan. A gardener here in Aqaba said to Kristina, "Of course I was against the war, but now I see pictures on TV showing happy Iraqis, so now I am happy for them and hope only for the best!"

Pass the Oud and Play the Nay

Knowing that the looting in Baghdad was continuing, our Egyptian taxi driver said, "No one knows what will happen or who will do what, but the people remain the people. For thousands of years we are simply trying to live in peace while the leaders are unpredictable. No one can stop these wars. The people, like you and me, are helpless."

Our music and dance continue by the Red Sea. Since tea, not alcohol, is the beverage of choice, the party will continue in a deeply considerate and polite atmosphere.

When we arrived in Jordan our taxi driver and another Jordanian passenger didn't even try to analyze the world with these two mysterious American characters named Cameron and Kristina. Once they discovered that we sing and play Arabic music, they simply wanted to sing with us. With the bond of musical friendship established, it felt, as always, like we were part of the same family.

History has been written. We must not remain stuck in obsolete viewpoints. The forces toward healing the wounds in Iraq must proceed as rapidly as possible. For this to be achieved, hatchets must be buried and new alliances

64

formed. However mistrustful of the American government's motives for attacking Saddam Hussein many of us may have felt, we must support co-operation and growth. The old concepts of "good and evil" can, hopefully, dissolve. With our united efforts and prayers we can move forward.

Can you find all five faces in this picture?

We have been creating friendships based on love through music in both America and the Arab world, all the while knowing that our Iraqi friends have themselves been divided on the merits of America's attack on Saddam Hussein's rule. Some of them see only evil in America's war, while others hope for a quick American victory over Saddam's regime so things may begin again with a fresh start. Many of them have lost family members to Saddam's executions.

"Six months from now things will be much better for the Iraqi people. We will hope for this," was another comment heard here in Jordan.

We have just spent the last two hours beside the waters of the Red Sea here in the Gulf of Aqaba, playing for thirty or forty dancing Arab and Bedouin young people. It all began when a tea vendor noticed my oud and invited us to play. There was much singing and dancing. I played the nay along with many local Bedouin melodies, and Kristina and I were both pulled to our feet to dance. We were also treated to lots of free tea.

Someone asked me where we were from and I replied, "America." I thought I detected a slight hesitation or look of astonishment before the hospitable exclamation: "you are welcome! Welcome to Jordan!" came forth. Maybe it was just my own feeling of sadness that caused me have this perception; I don't know.

We must now also turn our attention toward the Palestinian situation. Relying on all the old hatreds will not bring a better situation for the millions of living souls involved. Fresh and open-minded work is desperately needed.

Tomorrow we will travel north to Amman and, hopefully, visit with our Iraqi friend, Ali, and his family.

More New Friends in Aqaba.

Back to Amman

Sunday, April 13, 2003

We arrive back in Amman, the capitol of Jordan, after a four- or five-hour bus ride from Aqaba . Swarms of taxi drivers pounce on us as we extract our luggage from the bus. Kristina, offended at being treated like a newcomer, fends them off and leads us out onto the street. "I feel like walking, don't you?" she inquires. It feels like we need to reclaim our familiarity with the city by walking through it. "Sure, let's walk," I respond.

We eventually find the restaurant with the parakeets and their little egg. We enter and ask the owner about them. "The poor little fellow died. He didn't make it, but now they are busy making more eggs. This time, *insha'Allah...* (God willing) we will have babies!"

> *E-Mail from Ali:*
> *Subject: Urgent*
> *Date: Mon, 14 Apr 2003*
>
> *Cameron;*
> *I'm sorry. Today was a strange day to me. Anyway, I want a favor from you. Do you know any Medical institute that does any voluntary work? We have a child in Iraq. He is about to die if he doesn't get medical treatment. This child was bombed with his family. His family is all dead, and he is totally burned except for his face. He is suffering a lot, and his parts were cut off (arms, not sure about his legs). If you can get me in contact with any person who has the ability to help ASAP, I would consider this as a personal favor. Needless to say there are no drugs in Iraq to ease the pain.*   *Regards, Ali*

Mobilize medical help? How will we do this? We will see Ali soon.

We ate a bite of food and made our way to the Saraya Hotel, where we were greeted affectionately by Fayaz, the owner. This is one of the small hotels in which we had stayed a few months earlier.

It just so happened that many of the motley, international brigade known as the Human Shields were staying at this hotel. During the next few days we sat in on their story-swapping sessions. They were just coming out of Iraq in considerable numbers. We became acquainted with ten or 15 of them. They were from many different parts of the world and had stayed in Baghdad during the bombing. By announcing their presence and exact locations to the press and especially to the U.S. military, they hoped to discourage the targeting of those locations.

At the same time, the Jordanian Arabs working at the hotel were eager for us to sing and play, so we brought the oud and sang for a couple of hours with them downstairs.

The next day, still settling into the hotel and Amman, we did a few errands, called our Iraqi friends, talked further with various Human Shield volunteers, and yielded to local pressure to once again spend the evening playing Arabic music in the hotel.

E-Mail from Ali:
Subject: RE: Urgent
Date: Tue, 15 Apr 2003

Why don't you come and visit us? I know I'm a lazy person but it's mid-month to me: the time to make bills for my clients. This is why I'm a bit busy, although this is not an excuse. I have no phone to call out on. I can receive calls, but not dial out as I haven't paid the bill yet.   *Regards, Ali*

Today is my birthday. Kristina buys a piece of cake for me in a little restaurant to finalize our roasted chicken and rice meal. We visit the Monzer Hotel across town where members of Voices in the Wilderness congregate. There I had met Kathy Kelly, founder of Voices in the Wilderness, last December; she had attempted to help us get into Iraq a few months earlier. Our invitation by the Baghdad Musicians' Association had not been enough. Saddam Hussein's government had kept us out, denying our visas.

Back in Amman, Jordan, we hear that the bombing is decreasing in Iraq. "The Iraqi people would love you," we hear again and again from Jordanian friends.

Not everyone understands or sympathizes with our attempts to bridge cultural differences by reaching out and learning the other culture's popular music so that we can enjoy and feel something sweet and visceral together. The politicians understand political or military approaches. The anti-war activists understand marches, demonstrations, sit-ins, civil disobedience, information publication and petitions. But the music lovers on the streets of the world understand what we are doing. It is more easily understood with the heart than with the mind.

We meet Nassim, who helps run the Monzer Hotel. He offers to set up a car and driver to deliver us to Baghdad, 500 miles away, for a reasonable price: something less than a quarter of the $2000 price the high-end journalists had been paying. Our imaginations are sparked. We had not expected to make it into Baghdad with the war going on, but now it seems that the fighting and bombing is tapering off. We tell Nassim we will be thinking about this possibility.

During the evening we are invited to attend a house concert featuring a young female Jordanian singer accompanied by an oud player who specializes in Lebanese styles.

Back at our hotel later, accompanied by some new Jordanian friends we had met at the concert, we listened to a story told by David Lynn, an American Human Shield who, after being a soldier in Vietnam, eventually turned his energies to anti-war activities. He, along with all the other Human Shields we have talked with, denied that they were ever, as claimed by the media, requested by Saddam's regime to go to certain locations.

He was in a location in northern Baghdad, which was one of the last portions of the city to be taken by the U.S. Marines. Deciding at some point to go out on his own and see what was happening, he walked some 15 kilometers through the northern parts of the city. What he saw were the dead bodies of many civilians who had been shot while walking or driving. Afraid to leave the shelter of their houses, their families were just now emerging to bury these bodies, which had laid out in the sun for several days by that time. David witnessed these burials taking place, in spite of being exposed to gunfire several times himself. There was no record-keeping involved; no one could have counted all these deaths.

Our new Jordanian friends stayed at our hotel to listen for an hour or two and then took their leave. We had thought perhaps to play more music, but on this night the discussions were paramount.

Wednesday, April 16th, 2003:
Up at 8:00 a.m., we speed over to the Ministry of the Interior, as Nassim had suggested, to try to gain papers from the Jordanian government to be allowed into Iraq. After the fall of Saddam's government, the Jordanians instituted a policy of allowing only journalists to pass the border. We are, in some sense, journalists, but we don't have official press cards.

The Ministry of the Interior refers us to the pressroom at the Inter-Continental Hotel. Instead of presenting press cards, we present an introduction written in Arabic, which has been gradually evolving with the help of several Arabic friends. The Jordanian officials read this, looking at us inquisitively. We sing them a piece of a song in Arabic. Suddenly they smile broadly. It is as if they all at once understand who we are. A woman named Maha invites us to her desk and arranges a contact for us at the border so that we will be given permission to pass into Iraq. Everyone in the pressroom now seems cheerful and smiling.

We head back to the hotel to meet Stefa, a Canadian Human Shield. She has invited us to go with her to meet a wealthy female Jordanian peace activist. Once seated in a local restaurant, she brings out an Arabic newspaper which contains the news that the Human Shields organization had been infiltrated by the CIA. According to this article, the CIA worked inside Iraq to pay off the Republican Guard so they wouldn't put up a fight.

The current belief is that Saddam's high echelon of family and ministers arranged a secret surrender with the CIA and were whisked out of the country to some safe haven. There are various versions of this story, I'm sure, but the point which our Jordanian peace activist friend is trying to make to Stefa is that being associated with the Human Shields is no longer an honorable thing in the Arab street; it is now a suspect thing. Privately I congratulate myself on my decision to never associate myself with any organization or government.

We stop by the Monzer Hotel and tell Nassim that the plan to enter Iraq is a go. We have been permitted by the Jordanians to cross the border into Iraq.

Evening comes and we take a taxi across town to meet our Iraqi refugee friend Ali, his mother, Suaad, and his younger brothers, Haydar and Ahmed. We are very anxious to see them. One way or another, they are surviving. Ali follows a fairly strict set of Islamic rules. He doesn't like to accept help from us either, as this seems to offend his pride. We had to read the ingredients on the box of chocolates we had brought for his mother to make certain that there was no brandy and no pork fat in the chocolate. He eventually agreed that his mother should accept the gift.

Later, Kristina presented his mother with a gold bracelet, a gift we had carefully calculated to be a way for us to get some form of money to them, to help them just in case of emergency. Ali immediately announced that they would not accept the present. "It's not for you!" I told him, laughing at his stubbornness, "it is for Suaad!"

That seemed to settle the issue and Kristina's gift to Suaad became a reality. They returned a gift to us: a series of psychic readings from Suaad, which addressed all our plans and ambitions, as well as the outlook for all our relatives.

Suaad had inherited from her mother a collection of seashells and other objects such as old door keys and other relics from their family's past. She also inherited the psychic gift from her mother, we are told. The next two hours were spent with Suaad tossing this double handful of relics into the air over a cloth and then reading their positions as they landed.

Several times they looked into our plan to enter Baghdad by interpreting these shells and could see only failure in this plan; even death could come to us if we were to try to make this trip. The outlook for all of our children seemed quite good, however, and information about our children's past and current struggles with growth and life seemed quite accurate.

Leaving at 2:30 a.m to return to our hotel, we found a long walk awaiting us in the cold, as there were no taxis in sight in that part of town. Eventually we reached a larger avenue and found a cab for the rest of the way.

That night I could not sleep. I lay awake until 7:00 a.m., digesting the various aspects of Suaad's readings. After one hour of semi-sleep, I rose from bed to begin a busy day, full of preparations for the trip to Baghdad. We had to carry our own water and food and be prepared to pay for things with small denominations of U.S. dollars. We spent part of the afternoon with Nassim at the Monzer Hotel, discussing all the arrangements regarding our driver. Only Iraqi drivers would be allowed into Iraq, and these Iraqi drivers and their vehicles were only allowed to enter and park in one place in Amman. We communicated our arrangement made at the press room at the Inter-Continental Hotel. We were to arrive to Al Ruwasheid, the last small town before the Iraqi border, and find a certain man named Mahjed at the Shat el Arab Hotel. There we would provide extra passport photos, and be given some kind of visa permitting us entry to Iraq.

We were able to contact Mahjed on Nassim's cell phone. He assured us he knew who we were from our friend, Maha, in the press room at the Inter-Continental Hotel, and that there would be no problem. The only thing was that he might not be there, in which case we were to find his brother, Ali. Nassim introduced us to our Iraqi driver's brother, a large man who assured us that everything would be fine.

We returned to the streets to finish our errands of preparation for the trip. We needed white cloth so that we would be able to wave white flags of truce toward the U.S. Marines if necessary. We also needed orange tape, to write "PRESS" and "TV" in large letters on the car, so we would not be suspected of being smugglers or infiltrators. We told Nassim to have the Iraqi driver take care of that part, as we didn't have a ready source for the orange tape. Nassim had told us to call him at 10:00 p.m. to find out where to meet our car and driver. He said we would be part of an armed caravan, departing early the following morning from the Iraqi border to travel together through the lawless and bandit-filled 300 miles of western Iraq desert. I asked Kristina if she was certain she wanted to make this trip with me. "It seems to be our path," she replied with no hesitation.

All the years I had spent traveling through the low-rent districts of South America, finding delightfully friendly folks around every corner (in spite of the repeated warnings from wealthy people and rival tribes that "surely I would be killed if I went there") came together to give me clear confidence now.

Armed with my musical instrument (my oud) and a handful of heartfully memorized Arabic songs, we would sing with the people on the streets of Baghdad, making our American nationality known, and trust in the music and the basic goodness of the common man.

After scrambling all evening with preparations, we called Nassim from our hotel at 10:00 p.m. He told us to hurry over to the Monzer Hotel; he would accompany us to the Iraqi car and driver from there.

Friday, April 18th, 2003:
By 12:30 a.m. we were headed out of Amman toward Iraq with Imad, our expansive, energetic and basically mono-lingual driver. I shifted all (still not much) of my knowledge of Arabic into the front of my brain and began getting to know him. Basic sentences take me a long time and a lot of brain strain to find ways to use my limited vocabulary as creatively as possible.

Imad seemed friendly and alert. He took turns initiating basic conversations in Arabic with Kristina and me. "How old are you?" we asked. He is 29, and has a wife, but no children. "God's will," he explained, adding that he had been to the doctor but either he or his wife was infertile. He seemed obviously quite sad about this.

After about three hours we arrived in Al Ruwasheid, found the Shat el Arab Hotel, but pounded on the doors to no avail. We found someone with a cell phone and tried the phone numbers. The two brothers had their phones turned off and were sleeping, we supposed. It was 4:00 a.m. Determining to wait for another hour or so, we thought to maybe grab a nap in the parked car.

Suddenly a large, female German doctor appeared, in the middle of some misunderstanding with her Jordanian drivers. I don't think she was aware that only Iraqi drivers were being allowed to cross into Iraq. She was very upset and hoping that she could ride with us, although she still didn't have her visa. Imad quickly concluded that she was "*majnoon* (insane)!"

There seemed to be no way to work things out with this big, angry doctor, so Imad sped off into the night toward the Iraqi border. "No, wait!" we told him. "We must find one of the brothers and get our visas!"

But Imad had decided to proceed. "We'll miss the armed convoy if we don't go now," he said. There never turned out to be any convoy, either armed or unarmed. Such is life.

74

Unable to convince him otherwise, we sped the last 50 miles to the border, where we entered into a tangled mass of Jordanian officials in various offices and behind various windows. Signs on the walls proclaimed in both Arabic and English: "The highway in Iraq is exceptionally dangerous. Jordan does not recommend traveling."

We would not be allowed entry without press cards, we were told. But we knew what to do. We produced our explanation about our musical mission, written in Arabic, and when they looked at us, we sang pieces of Arabic songs. Stunned, delighted and amazed, they told us to go around to the office in back to speak with the Captain. His bloodshot eyes told us that he had been on duty for too many nights and it didn't look like he was in a good mood. But again, once we sang the magic music, he burst into a broad smile and sent us back around to the front office where the stamps in our passports miraculously appeared—but not, of course, until we had sung one more song for everybody in the front office. We delivered a mini-concert to an increasingly delighted audience. Imad had done a good job, also, of leading us from one official to another, although at one point he had seemed ready to give up.

After we cross the Jordanian border and enter Iraq, we find that bomb craters have destroyed parts of the highway to Baghdad.

Into Iraq

After two hours of this musical 'negotiating', we were speeding across no man's land toward Iraq. "Enough with the Jordanians!" exclaimed Imad. "I don't like them! Too many rules!"

We approached a checkpoint manned by U.S. Marines. Imad, the ultimate horn-honking, aggressive taxi driver, tried to nose his way into the front of two lines of cars waiting to be checked by the Marines. "No, Imad," we told

Bombed truck: another one of many destroyed on this highway; a relic of the anonymous death and destruction of air attack.

It appeared that all aboard this Syrian Bus were killed, including many Russian diplomats on their way out of the war zone.

The remains of a bombed bridge reveal the destructive power of modern weaponry.

him, "this is not going to work with these guys." Soon we were escorted back to the end of the lines and made to wait our turn.

"Americans, huh," the Marine checking our passports muttered. "You guys must be crazy!"

Soon we were speeding down a divided highway made of concrete with metal guard rails between the lanes headed toward Baghdad. Iraq obviously had, at one time, the money to spend on highways much fancier than anything we had seen in Jordan. Soon, however, we were weaving around bomb craters punched into the concrete and passing the burnt husks of trucks, buses, cars and tanks.

Another bombed vehicle overturned
on the road to Baghdad.

Imad winced with pain as we passed each one. "And that bus there," he explained, "was not even Iraqi, it was from Syria!" We had read about the bombing of a Syrian bus in which several Russian diplomats died, along with ten or so other passengers.

Bedouin villages were visible on the distant horizon to the north. "They don't like to be close to the road," explained Imad. My curiosity was aroused and I wanted to visit. I wondered if they played some of the same songs we had heard in the desert from Hussein in southern Jordan, but now was obviously not the time for a visit.

We covered two or three hundred miles and passed the Euphrates River. Palm trees began to appear as water became part of the landscape. We passed clusters of burnt, overturned and abandoned Iraqi tanks, and more bombed trucks, buses, and cars. Other car and truck frames which had not been burnt were periodically visible beside the highway. "Ali Baba! Ali Baba!" exclaimed Imad, lamenting the thievery.

Eventually we realized that the looting, which has been publicized in Baghdad, extended out onto the highways. If your car runs out of gas or becomes otherwise inoperable here and you have to leave it, you will find all its working parts stripped and gone when you get back.

Baghdad

"Ali Baba!" screams Imad again as he points at the mobs of looters, thick on the streets and at their work as we wind our way into central Baghdad. We detour around the edges of what the press called 'the biggest anti-American demonstration yet'—a huge crowd of Iraqis holding anti-U.S. banners and occupying many city blocks.

Imad slips at high speed through the smoke-filled intersections. No electricity means no traffic lights. No government means no laws. Drivers making up their own rules. Imad makes up for the loss of order by leaning on the horn.

Six or eight of the nearby high-rise buildings have flames leaping out of their windows. No water means no putting out these fires. Who is torching this city? Why?

Baghdad: the city of burning buildings.

*We hope he gets it started! If he has to leave it,
it will become fair game for the looters.*

More burning buildings in Baghdad.

Knowing that our friend, Kathy Kelly is staying at the Al Fonar Hotel, we ask Imad to take us there. When we arrive, we find that it, along with the Palestine and Ishtar Hotels, is surrounded by U.S. Marines. This, it seems, is where the international corps of journalists are staying, and they are overflowing into Al Fonar. We must pass through a U.S. Marine checkpoint in order to enter the hotel.

*Al Fonar Hotel: we get the last room available
and then head out into the streets.*

We check into what is apparently the last unoccupied room, carry in our packs, food and water, turn around and head back out through the U.S. Marine checkpoint into the city, oud in hand.

Playing on the Streets of Baghdad: we find the same welcoming reception here which we had found in every other Arab-world city.

Life and hospitality go on for Iraqi street vendors.
We are offered tea and shishkabob as we sing.

This is the opportunity we, with our own style of international diplomacy, had been looking for. It didn't take long for the usual Arab-world scenario to unfold. Fifty yards down the street, past the last coils of U.S. Marine razor wire, a group of Iraqis point at my oud and ask us to play.

Excited to be back in familiar musical territory, I take the oud out of its case, and begin playing an Um Kolthoum song. "No, no!" someone shouts, "Saddam Hussein taught us not to like Um Kolthoum." I pass the oud to one of them who plays a *taqasim* (improvisation) in what seems to me to be the style of Farid al Atresh. It's then my turn again. I had been surprised by the rejection of the Um Kolthoum piece but decided to go ahead and sing something definitely Iraqi. I begin with a famous vocal and oud *mawal* (introduction) written by Iraqi composer Mohammed Al-Gobbanchi, and made famous by Syrian singer Sabah Fakhri.

Heads bob and move in time to the music as we all sing a favorite old Iraqi song. Smoke from burning buildings fills the air in the background.

This hits the perfect note, it seems, with the crowd. There is a gradual period of attentive silence. People are gradually realizing that I really do know this song. Eyes close, heads bob and shake with appreciation. The afternoon begins to dissolve into music. I hear voices joining in the song with me. Someone gently and lovingly adjusts the wayward hairs in my eyebrows as I sing. Tea is being made and offered.

Having shared this favorite old Iraqi song, I felt the welcoming energy in the crowd deepen. It felt like we were surrounded by friends and soul-mates once again. This happens so easily. "We need to see more people like you!" I am told by a man who enthusiastically embraces my shoulders.

A man in a tan *galibiya* (traditional Arab gown) who had been listening appreciatively approached us. "Since you are Americans, I would like to send a message to Bush with you: the Americans must leave! We will build

"Take a message to Bush..."
A political moment.

a new government ourselves! Government coming from the outside is not good! We will kill them!" Meanwhile, a few feet away, two men are telling Kristina the opposite message: "We are thankful to Bush for ridding us of Saddam Hussein."

An excited young man approaches me and introduces himself as the author of a book about *maqamat* (Arabic musical scales), and very enthusiastically offers to take us to a music school to meet a great master oud player whom he respects. He is apparently oblivious to the fact that the city around us is in flames. We suggest that maybe another time would be better.

We pass by the Tigris River thinking there might be a nice spot for more singing there, but the Marines are using the park beside the river for a camp. Walking the small side streets we see nothing but deserted apartments and streets filled with debris from the looting. A few small boys play with a soccer ball amongst the twisted remnants of broken building materials.

The entrance to the U.S.-controlled area was later called the "green zone."

Returning toward the main streets, we come to the circle called *al-Firdos*, or Paradise Square, where the whole world watched on TV as Marines used a tank to help Iraqis pull over a huge statue of Saddam. A man driving by in his car spots the oud and inquires if we play it. "Yes, we are Americans who love Arabic music and who play the oud and sing," I tell him in Arabic. He parks his car and we begin singing for him and others who randomly approach. The pedestal with fragments of Saddam's demolished statue stands in the background as we sing Abd el Halim's *Sawah*, a song about a man who misses his love, and walks for days and weeks like a stranger in a strange land.

As I sing, I scan the eyeballs in the crowd. They are so happy to see us singing! We announce several times, as people inquire, that we are Americans who love Arabic music. Some of the eyes are uncertain at first, but not for long as people melt into the songs and join in the singing. The man with the car says he plays the oud also and is anxious to take us with him in his car to his house to play music. He, too, seems to find his encounter with us

88

more important than the fact that the city is in flames. It takes five or six polite declinations from us to postpone this offer until another time. We had just read in a newspaper in Jordan that Iraqi families had been killed for inviting Americans into their homes. I add his phone number to my list of musicians to contact in the future.

Al Firdus, or "Paradise" Square
The pedestal of the fallen Saddam statue is in the background.

At this point, as I later calculated, I had enjoyed only one hour of sleep in the last fifty-seven hours. Feeling groggy with exhaustion, I suggest taking a break in the hotel room, but Kristina is eager to continue on the streets.

Wanting to get every angle on what's happening, she asks a Marine behind the hotel if we could interview him. "Not while I'm on post," he replies. "But if you go down this street, there is a little place for coffee where Marines hang out, but I don't know if I'd recommend it; we've got snipers on the roofs of all these hotels."

We are searched by other Marines before being allowed to proceed. We ask for the location of this coffee shop and a higher-ranking Marine says, "You mean one of my men suggested that you could go there? He should not have said that. Which man is he?" the Marine asks. "I don't know," replies Kristina, "with the uniforms you all look the same!" We proceed through coils of razor wire down the street, but are told we cannot go toward the coffee shop.

"Do You Play that Oud?
Come to My House!"
The Palestine Hotel, a favorite for Western
journalists, is in the background.

*Young Marine whom we tried to interview:
unfortunately he was under orders not to
talk to anyone.*

*The Marines have occupied this one small area
around the big hotels.*

Leaving the area cordoned off by the Marines, we re-enter the city and find a restaurant which, surprisingly, is open and we eat some chicken and rice. Some friendly Iraqis at a table next to us give us a can of Pepsi. The restaurant could only sell some less-tasty Iraqi equivalent.

"What snipers do you suppose he was referring to?" I asked Kristina.
"Well, *Iraqi* snipers, I assumed," she replied.
"I thought maybe he meant *Marine* snipers," I suggested.

*Downtown Baghdad: Iraqis carry on
as well as possible with 'life as usual.'*

Finishing our meal, we walked some more. We witnessed several instances of Marines brandishing weapons and shouting things like, "Move that fucking truck and move it quick, asshole!" screamed in English at uncomprehending Iraqi civilians. We witnessed other Marines going out of their way to say "*Salaam we Aleikum* (Peace be with you)" to Iraqis passing through their checkpoints. We wander back toward the hotel. I'm groggier and groggier with exhaustion.

We hear what sounds like a gunshot. Kristina backs behind a concrete wall away from the center of the street. It doesn't occur to me to worry, for some reason, but I back into the more protected area also. No one out on the street seems to pay any attention. The shots cease, so we continue walking.

Hundreds of international journalists throng the spaces around the Palestine and Ishtar hotels, both nearby. We walk among them. They peer out from the rooftops with the latest high tech portable video gear. Grim-faced and red-eyed, they go about their story-writing with cigarettes lit, adding to the smoke.

We just demonstrated, to my own satisfaction at least, that America could have invaded Iraq with battalions of our own citizens trained to play ouds and sing just a few songs in Arabic so that we could be falling in love. But the journalists, for the most part anyway, don't seem to be interested in or able to focus on this idea. That we are all victims of obviously unsuccessful, traditional approaches to problem-solving based on blind beliefs in one-sided verbal arguments is not an idea yet on their tables. Or if it is, it has been pre-empted by the bombing.

We pass back through the Marine checkpoint. I show my oud to one of the Marines. "Wow! Cool! It's kind of like a bass, huh?" he asks. "Yeah," I reply, "it's an instrument they play a lot around here."

We return to our hotel room; I lie down on the bed and pass out for two hours. Opening my eyes in the late afternoon, I announce to Kristina that I'm ready to go back out. She is feeling worse now, however—the smoke from the burning city is making her sick to her stomach and giving her a bad headache.

I went down to Kathy Kelly's room and we greeted each other. Nothing was surprising at this point to either one of us and it felt very natural to find ourselves in the same place once again. Her organization, Voices in the Wilderness, was founded to witness and report from inside Iraq about the effects of the sanctions and the war on the lives of Iraqi people. Kathy had been here at the Al Fonar Hotel with a few other VITW members for the last two months or so and had, like the Human Shields, been unwilling to leave when the bombing started. She is an activist with a track record of having succeeded in walking the fine line required by Saddam Hussein's government to be allowed entry, although they had had to live under constant surveillance by their Iraqi 'minders' in order to do their reporting. They had deliberately tried to avoid being associated with the title 'Human Shield', but fines are now being imposed on Kathy and her organization by the U.S. government for having broken the sanctions by bringing medical supplies into Iraq.

Fully aware that it would not be easy to find a reasonably-priced ride back to Jordan any time soon and facing the impending departure flight soon scheduled for our return to the U.S., we accepted an opportunity to ride back to Amman in a car with her the next morning.

Once again we wind our way out through the burned and looted sections of Baghdad. Today there seem to be fewer flames leaping out of the tall high-rise buildings, and the smoke is clearing a little bit. We sing Arabic music with our Iraqi driver and enjoy the company of those who are riding with us.

When we arrived back at the Jordanian border, the police there recognized us and again requested songs. We obliged by giving another mini-concert and their smiles grew as we sang.

Back in Amman, we spend another evening visiting Ali, his mother and his two brothers. Suaad cooks a fabulous dinner for us. We discuss the readings from the shells, which had predicted that we should not go to Baghdad. We agree that the reading had been somewhat accurate, perhaps meaning that our trip to Baghdad would be difficult. Suaad suggests that her reading had meant that, although it had obviously been okay for us to go to Baghdad for a few days, it would not have been good for us to stay for a long time.

We show them our photos from Baghdad. We discuss the question of who it is that is setting all the fires. Haydar agrees that the best guess is that the looters, many of whom are very poor and very young, just get carried away with the destruction and, after looting, light the buildings on fire. He speculates it's something that teenage boys would do. Ali thinks that many of the looters must be from Kuwait. At this point it doesn't seem that Ali and his family have any plans to ever return to Iraq.

Outdoing us once again in the hospitality department, Suaad gives Kristina an exquisitely beaded vest made by a favorite aunt, as well as some perfume. We will see them next trip, whenever that is, *insha'Allah*.

94

Back in Cairo, we watch as an Egyptian friend, who had lived in Baghdad for ten years, bursts into tears when we show him our photos from Iraq.

Back in America, we begin giving the first of what turn out to be hundreds of presentations about this heartful world we have been drawn to explore. We find ourselves invited and welcomed into congregations of many denominations and groups of many types where people are curious to learn from us.

Millions of people are praying for some new rays of hope in the Middle East.

What does it mean 'to pray'? Perhaps prayer is the natural state of pure connection which unites all beings in compassion *when the element of fear is gone.*

Can we not all feel our sense of compassionate connection with others ebb and flow, as our *fears* come and go?

A friend of ours in Colorado has created a non-profit organization, Musical Missions of Peace, devoted to *overcoming fear* in this world.

It is by becoming *familiar* with each other that our fears of each other can be erased.

And it is by singing together that we feel an instant *familiarity.*

To be *familiar* is to feel that we are part of the same *family.*

Postscript

We have made two more trips back to the Arab world since returning to America from Baghdad.

Later, in the fall of 2003, we were invited by the Egyptian coordinators of a fundraiser for the construction of a children's cancer hospital in Cairo to be the only non-Arab musicians to perform in the Cairo stadium. We did this for an audience of 60,000 Egyptians. Since we played popular Egyptian music, we experienced the gratification of hearing the crowd singing along with us. We were part of an all-day line-up of musicians which included the top Egyptian pop music stars.

With the concert behind us, we used the opportunity of being back in the Arab world again to explore parts of Syria and, of course, found the same hospitality in Damascus, Aleppo and Lattakia. We also played and sang with children in Jaramana, a huge Palestinian refugee camp just outside of Damascus.

We returned once again to the Arab world in the autumn of 2004. This time we divided between Syria, Lebanon, Jordan and Egypt, deepening connections with many friends and exploring some additional new places. Televison coverage of our bridge-building work went out in Arabic-language media to many millions of viewers all over the world.

Returning to the U.S. in the spring of 2005, we resumed our on-the-road series of multimedia presentations about the Arab world. As of this writing, we have driven more than 40,000 miles through the U.S. and flown many more miles to deliver our presentations. We have found Americans to be generous in offering to help support our work by making donations through Musical Missions of Peace.   December, 2005

*Cameron and Kristina's audience of 60,000
in the Cairo Stadium in the autumn of 2003.*

*We were honored to be part of a benefit performance
which included many Egyptian pop stars to help raise
funds for Childrens Cancer Hospital project "57357."*

*Cameron and Kristina's home on the road in
America from 2002 through 2005.
The trailer was finally destroyed in June,
2005, when high winds caused it to hit a
bridge on Interstate 5 in central California.*

Historical Overview

At the time we went to Baghdad as musical ambassadors, the stage was set for a major paradigm shift in how world diplomacy can be conducted.

Gone are the days when armies can rush in and conduct a bloody purge of terror under the cloak of secrecy. The modern age of internet-based journalism has arrived. Anyone with a digital camera can publish the story in spite of the best efforts at censorship. In order to truly win a battle under the glare of this light, the campaign must be conducted somehow simultaneously on the ground and in the minds and hearts of a watching world!

World leaders are gradually becoming aware that winning wars must now include a public relations element, which must promote the effort to a global public increasingly aware of egalitarian ideals. This is more than "might makes right." We hear talk about "winning and maintaining the moral high ground."

The U.S. has enjoyed a long-term, world-wide image as champions of democracy. Over-reliance on the durability of this image can cause leaders to over-step their gamble that world public opinion will remain sided with the U.S. The U.S. strategy is unraveling under the glare of public outrage at the human costs of the invasion of Iraq. A great moment was missed.

Our Iraqi friends told us the Iraqi people would fight the U.S. invasion for however many years or decades it might take to drive out what they perceive as yet another colonial occupation. It took decades to drive out the British, but they succeeded. Yes, a great moment was missed.

During the time when Washington was sounding the drumbeats of the impending war, an entirely new type of strategy could have been launched which would have created a win-win situation for all. It would have been hailed as a giant step forward for humanity and for American leadership. America, as the 'champion of democracy', was perfectly suited to institute this change, which could have happened under the glare of focused world media. The Arab world, with its powerful and ancient tradition of hospitality as the bottom line, was the perfect place for this experiment to unfold. One hundred thousand young Americans could have been trained to sing popular Iraqi music.

Remember, *the Iraqi people were never our enemy.* The U.S. has now made them an enemy by militarily invading their homes and exterminating tens of thousands of them with unthinkably lethal weaponry. But can you imagine the incredible wave of inspiration which would have swept the whole planet if, instead of invading Iraq with more weapons of mass destruction, the U.S. had invaded Iraq with music?

The hearts of Iraqi people would have been instantly won over, because we would have been singing *their* songs as an offering of personal respect.

The existing infrastructure, instead of being destroyed, could have been saved and then improved. Existing leadership could have been inspired to court the favor of world-wide public opinion. The whole evolution of power structures in Iraq could have been defined by America as the leaders of a new politics of love. No Iraqi leader could have afforded to attack an army of unarmed musicians. New cooperative ventures to re-distribute power inside Iraq could have resumed once again with the support of the West. The new millennium would have been ushered in properly—as it could have been—and the fuel of hatred would have evaporated from the platforms of all would-be terrorists.

Because the ancient music of the Arab world is at the foundation of so much of their ancient wisdom and spirituality, fundamentalists would have been deflated. A new modern light-handed Arabic Islamic energy would have been born and it would have been admirable in both the East and the West.

The waves of these successes could have set a new precedent for Planet Earth, which could have provided a new, healthier model for other parts of the globe, countries struggling to adjust borders drawn hastily by selfish, occupying powers.

In the words of a Mexican man with family in both Mexico and the U.S., "I don't cross the border—the border crosses me!" His statement refers to the fact that his Native American ancestors have been roaming Central and North America for many thousands of years.

Our extensive travels have shown us that people all over the world greet each other first with love. Try it. Buy a ticket and wander the globe. If that is not possible, learn a few notes of a popular Arabic song and surprise your local Syrian restaurant owner. Or at least go in and say "hi" and establish an open-ended friendship. Escape the industry of fear disguised as 'security'. There is a much more welcoming world out there awaiting those who choose to explore, and learn their neighbors' music.

In our *selfish* moments, the discovery that We are All One comes as a *threat*.

In our *generous* moments, the discovery that We are All One comes as a *great relief*.

Which direction will we choose to go?

A Sea of E-Mail

As we travel, we are in touch with thousands of people by e-mail. The presence of Internet Cafes in almost all cities and towns makes this easy. The following messages, which are selected from the many we received as we traveled in 2002 and 2003, give an historical sense of the "sea of public opinion" in which we were floating at that time.

****

Whew!
I've been so moved by the stories that you've been sending out, and then the pictures! Wow. They made me cry. I hope more and more people will come to realize that it's not the people who want to fight, but the governments. I'm just awed and inspired by what you two are doing. I'm honored to be your friend.
Peace and loads of love

****

Hello Darlings! I am resonating with appreciation for your courageous and compassionate mission... Every day you both are smiling and singing in my mind and heart. Thank you so much for keeping us posted on your adventures - this morning's photos make it even more real for us. It has been clear to me for some time that people all over the globe in every country simply want to live and love and be well. Your mission is that which needs to be happening to awaken the reality of our oneness. Those who want war are just a few. It is time for people to join together everywhere in claiming the right to a peaceful existence. The work-play of your musical bridge between our cultures is vitally important at this time. Thank you again for taking it upon yourselves to represent the consciousness that is the force of peace. I am so grateful to be your friend.

****

****

It's wonderful to have good news from the Middle East!! The stories have been great. We need an army of fairies to carry them to every American home. I can feel you guys and see the pictures of you boogeying down in these little music shops. Good on you!! Reminds me of when I was in Istanbul at the end of Ramadan, and what a lovely dinner and celebration was served, with all the children rough-housing and huge extended families gathering.

****

I read your words and my eyes are not dry any more. Quickly. Please keep your letters and add more and more and more. These are great stories. Please keep writing.

****

It's good to hear tales of your journey. Music is the most wonderful thing to share with people - it truly is a universal language.

****

Thank you for your gentle, compassionate and courageous voyage -- and your punctual progress reports about it. I must add that the interview you granted us here at Free Speech TV is also really inspiring, infused with each of the above mentioned qualities we will definitely be running it in our "Mobile-Eyes on Creating Peace." I'm sure we will still manage to create an impressive document celebrating your humanity and commitment to peace and we will certainly end the piece with your website address, so viewers across the nation who are moved to respond to your gesture can do so a safe and profound continuation to you both, saving the world with each step .

****

What a wonder to receive your up-to-the-minute reports! Thank you so much for sharing your adventure, for taking the time out to write to us. Any glimpses of dance? I'm following you all in my mind and heart, and my classes are cheering you on. They know you from your 4:01 a.m. CD. Much love to you both, prayers for safe and happy travels.

****

****

Blessings on you'all , what we don't understand is hard to tolerate, you are helping more to understand -- the presence of Faith in the very air --Respect of traditions -- We must continue to stand in awe in the presence of the spirit -- no matter what it is called.
Blessings to you!!

****

Thank you for all your updates. My heart goes with you. Three years ago I was doing similar terrain on a bicycle. Thirty-three years ago by hitch hiking and walking. I did make it to Iraq but the visa was a big problem even then. I had to shuttle between Amman and Beirut twice. Then across the desert in trucks. But it was all very worth it. I hope you can stop the war.

****

Right on!!!....WRITE ON!!!!!!!!!!..................

****

WOW!
Sounds like you two are having a wonderful experience! I sure wish our leaders could see things in a better light. You are doing the right thing! War is not the answer -- obviously, religious wars have torn up the earth--pretty damned ironic, isn't it, as all religions... revere life... Jackasses... Keep on truckin'! You are in my thoughts and in our music.

****

I love what you are doing there and here about the non-judgmental and open way you are relating to the people you meet.

****

Go baby go!

****

****

You guys, I am very impressed with your travel stories! Both of you are great writers. I'd like very much to write an article about your adventures if you'd let me. I'm so impressed that I've been forwarding your words on to my family, and raving about your gumption and faith in the universe. Do you mind if I record what you're doing for posterity? And perhaps send it out to a few magazines? I think the world needs to know about what you're doing. I figure that I have the time, and your words really inspire me. If any money comes in I'll scoop off like 10 percent and give the rest to you and your travel fund!

****

Very much appreciated receiving your first letter from Amman, Jordan. Looking forward to hearing more. I have experienced the call to prayer, in Java, also during Ramadan...and also in different places in India, just part of daily life. I really like it...it is beautiful and haunting...and, no matter who you are, it calls you to the moment... I love you,

****

Even without you asking I was preparing myself to try something for you case! I knew it. What I can do is to call someone who knows musicians in Baghdad and to see if they are willing to invite you. You have to tell me how this should work, i.e. the logistics of the way the Iraqi visa could be issued etc. I need to know so I can explain the situation. Well, have fun in Amman. Will be in touch if I have some contacts for you.

****

I would like to be put on the list please!
Thanks!

****

I will send you a healing to keep you in the "languaging rigor and zest to learn and grow in your communications in Arabic" So as to give you more opportunities to speak and connect with these wonderful people. And a healing for Kristina to keep singing the inspiration of the goddess to draw folks in - so that they will find out what you two are all about. Big hugs to you both. So, much gratitude that you

106

are on this journey---and that you are both on this planet!!! Man, you could have picked any planet to be on but you chose ours---yee haw!! Much love

****

This sounds so wonderful. I am so proud of both of you and would love to meet you Kristina. You are absolutely living your love and commitment to peace. Thanksgiving. Please keep sending the updates, and stay safe.

****

Thanks for the reports. It reminds me so much of when I visited Amman about 10 years ago, and was overwhelmed with the consistent friendliness, honesty, generosity, and genuine-ness of everyone I met. I've traveled very extensively in most countries in the world, and have never had such a strikingly positive impression of people.

****

It is Thanksgiving here in the states and I send you blessings. I appreciate tales of your wanderings and pray that your journey is safe. I know it will bring healing to many. I await more news.

****

****

Great stories, Cameron and Kristina. Make peace and music and be careful - we need you two back!

****

"May the long time sun shine upon you, All love surround you; And the pure light within you guide your way on."
 -the Incredible String Band
Vaya con Dios!

****

****

bravobravobravo!
Great to hear your news... looking forward to more!!!
Keep it rolling, and rocking, of course!!!

****

I feel so deeply moved and Honored to receive such intimate accounts of your majestic Journey to bring Peace to all beings. Thank you so very much for taking the time to write to us so eloquently about your first moments in Jordan. You are the true Peacemakers.
With sincere and heartfelt appreciation and gratitude,

****

Your accomplishments are very much in line with the objectives of my Austin-based band, Atash. We hope to help build bridges in cultural relations through music, especially during the current political climate in the world at large.

****

I so look forward to every report from you. The spirit of the music will unite you and it has. Truly language conceptions can be places for us to stuff our fears but music makes us dance, gives us courage to step out of time and into a place more transcendent. Be well,

****

I am loving hearing from you on your trip. It gives me such hope and comfort that the ways of peace are active in the world. Thank you both.

****

Why would anyone stay in the states if they had a chance to get out!
My love and blessings go with you wherever you go.

****

****

I've loved receiving your emails with news of your awesome goodwill journey!
****

Great, great, GREAT!!!!! way to go !!!!
Cheers and love and encouragement and blessings

****

Reading your emails and looking at the photos makes me all tear chokey backey.
You guys are putting my hundred bucks to good use as I expected!

****

HEY, GREAT PHOTOS!!!!! Keep up the good vibes!!!!
LOTS AND LOTS OF LOVE!!!

****

I love that you are there bringing light and love to the world. May there be peace
on earth and may it begin with me!!!

****

Thanks for sharing your trip with me. I've taken the liberty of sharing one of your
emails to the music newsletter, as I'm sure some of your acquaintances and fans
in Puerto Vallarta will love to hear about your trip.

****

'Once again we play a song of Um Kolthoum, the Egyptian super-goddess of the
Arab world...'
Only a super-goddess might hold off the super-power gone berserk.
I think she was there the night you played CU's Old Main.
Best wishes...

****

****

You are doing a fabulous job - keep it up. What you are doing in Amman is just a prelude, there is much more to be done and you can do it. Keep up the hope and the insistence on getting your visas. Your motives & goals are great, and there is a way to get there.

****

I really enjoy your report on the music. You fit the scene and are not shy to play wherever you like. No ties or bow tie and no problems. Just make the kids happy and let them see two Americans play Arabic music and they (the kids) will never forget you both. Maybe they will be inspired and start learning music. Who knows! Take care and we pray for you.

****

It's amazing getting your e-mails. I truly honor and am impressed by your undertaking. It must be difficult, glorious, and amazing. I pray that your wonderous journey continue as long as you both feel inclined to be there and that when you return, you both have a sense of completion and satisfaction. It's sad to me that such circumstances even need to exist, but that's my trip. Anyway, blessings, be safe, have fun, and listen deeply! Blessings

****

Cameron, the only words that come to mind are 'thank you'. Thank you for going, thank you for sending back your wonderful chronicles. I find it very inspiring. Thank you! I look forward to every next installment.

****

Kristina, just say the word & I'm here. Prayers work & the world is ripe...

****

110

****

I wish I could see photos, you paint such a beautiful picture! It is exciting to me in the amount of love you are putting out on this adventure. Cameron, you'd be proud, I stayed up till 4 am jammin' with my friends. We played saz and frame drum and singing bowl and chimes... Ah, what a night.

****

I seems like I have known you for a very long time. I read your peace journey article and now maybe others who read it will join you in song and prayer for peace in Palestine and in Iraq... Music is the soul of life and inner harmony. With a song in my heart, I wish you both much success on your music and songs for peace and harmony in this world in 2003!
HAPPY NEW YEAR 2003.

****

May your path be filled with blessings to be shared with all the people you are meeting. You are creating a path of love, light, and music that represents the best of human possibilities; I hope more people are inspired by your example and will undertake small and large efforts to bring peace and understanding.

****

What adventure, what a way to connect with our brothers and sisters. I so love to hear about what you are doing, and thank you, thank you, for showing the world another kind of American.

****

Thank you, thank you, thank you for your emails. My heart bleeds for the Palestinians.

****

****

I consume your writings with glee, awe, and tremendous respect (not to mention a tad of jealousy!)...

You are utilizing the gift of music towards it's highest purpose, of spreading joy and building bridges towards peace, understanding and hope-in a way that transcends politics- at a time when the forces of destruction and despair seem to be closing in from all directions. I truly am scared for our world, with the twin devils of war and environmental ruin seeming to encroach ever closer to all of our doors. Here is the USA we have felt too sheltered and impervious to what the rest of the world experiences. The human stories and photos you share with us are so wonderful and help to rekindle the feeling that we are one big human family sharing one big spaceship earth that will need all of our love and care to survive and thrive...

****

I am so thankful that the two of you have the courage and tenacity to go through with this. Perhaps in time I will also be able to join in similar peace efforts. I wish to say that I am a bit ashamed of myself. When last we saw each other I was so busy telling you to be careful that I forgot to mention that I am behind you doing this. I myself feel the same way and if all works well, I may also get a chance to spread peace through this wonderful music.

****

Believe me C&K, I interrupted my work in order to read your letter. Thanks for visiting in Ramallah and thanks for seeing the Israeli "art work" at the compound of the Arafat. The Israelis describe him as the devil and blame him for all the killing of Israelis. Excessive smoking and drinking and drug use result in cancer and death. That's exactly what more than 35 years of Israeli occupation to Palestinian land and mind does after all. Cancer, cancer, cancer. America has to stop the cancer because it allowed it for a long time. The occupation will end because no occupation has ever lived. The more it stays the more devastation it will bring to both. Fortunately, many Israelis know this fact and they are on the real peace camp together with their Palestinian friends. Thank you for your efforts in eating one meal in Ramallah and talking to one man and one woman in the great city Ramallah. No to the Israeli occupation of Palestine. Freedom and life to the brave Palestinians and Israelis who want to live side by side.

****

****

How are you, I hope that you enjoyed in Ramallah, and I hope you will come back and meet you again It was pleasure to meet you in that night and listened to your beautiful songs.

From your new friends in Ramallah

****

Peace be with you!

Thanks for sharing your courageous travel accounts, pictures and the courageous light of your hearts! Your accounts expand my insights and understanding of life in Arab countries. Hopefully, this can also add to understanding and recognition of our shared humanity. Your music always brightens up my Heart & Soul. May Allah's grace and infinite compassion, always travel well with you!

****

What great joy it was to read! Especially since I am inundated on my e-mail with daily news from Palestine which is bleaker and bleaker all the time. Thank you for the great work. I would love to continue receiving news of you- will you please add me to your list-serve? And I will be so happy to share news of what you are doing with my fellow artist-activists in Seattle, which is where I live, though I am currently in Santa Fe, eventually on my way to Turkey for three weeks. Happy New Year. I hope you get into Iraq. Does Amy Goodman know about you? She should.

Salaam again. Salaam always-

****

I wonder if you had time to enjoy Christmas and get a little weight for over eating stuffed Turkey. Well, since you are jumping from one town to another, I will attack the Turkey on your behalf. A few friends are sharing Christmas with us, after dinner, they were so excited hearing about your adventure.

****

I wish I was in Palestine with you and my people to sing for peace, love and joy in this world. I went to school in Ramallah when I was a child and with my uncles and aunts in the town of Beitunia, which next to Ramallah. At least you made the

Christians seem happier and brighter for people who truly dream of peace, in the the Holy Land.
Blessings and thanks for the translation.

****

Your words relating your experience with Ali are incredibly touching. The story is amazing. LOVE PREVAILS!!!!!!!!

****

We want to thank you for your e-mails and photos from Jordan. Your talents and skills are clearly appreciated there and your message of peace is shared by many around the world. I spoke to my friends the other day regarding your adventure and mission. They indicated that your strength, courage and energy are recognized and that you are receiving special spiritual guidance and protection. We look forward to your updates. We are all praying for you. Happy Holidays! Happy New Year! Pray Peace

****

I would like to thank you for bringing the harmony of music to build bridges of understanding and compassion for those whose voices are not heard or listened to. I commend you both on your peace efforts, especially in the Middle East. As a Palestinian American, I support your peaceful efforts to bring harmony and hope for a brighter, peaceful future to those who are suffering daily and yet, their voices go unheard. You are the bridge over troubled waters!
Blessings of peace,
Merry Christmas & A Very Peaceful and joyous New Year 2003!

****

Your letters are the highlight of my day.....the whole western world should see them. Blessings to you both with your great open hearts.

****

I saw you on FSTV! Good luck on your travels!

****

114

****

Was your trip planned to conclude these days? Did you plan to stay there for a longer time or you are going as scheduled. The West Bank is a mess and you will hate to see our people struggle for their basic humanitarian needs. But, if you need to see what it is like and why all this fuss is about you have to meet the local Palestinians in Jenin and Nablus and other cities. Then you will be an expert in the issue. One has to be very strong to see things and react (verbally) regardless the government's position. I understand that the weather is very tough right now. Are you warm enough? Take care and enjoy your remaining time.

****

Kristina, I just wanted to let you know how your stories have touched me. Thanks you so much for including me in your community. I have thought of you often experiencing such a different culture and being so open to learning everything it has to offer.

****

Cameron & Kristina I have been enjoying reading your several e-mails about your trip to the Middle East.

We are now working and living in Dubai, a very progressive and modern city with all the tradition and old culture of the Arab and non Arab Middle East, and with around 164 nationalities living here together in peace and harmony.

We are very happy for you on this opportunity of extending your love and under-standing to other people, especially to the down-trodden. We thank you for being what you are in your offering of hope to this Planet and to its clinging survivalists in the over all human family.

Please keep in touch for possible arranged visit to play to the people of Dubai. We could arrange it for I have strong desire for the people in Dubai to enjoy your music like we enjoyed back in Denver.

Just this last time we attended your performance was in Boulder Library when you joined in with the Palestinian maestro violinist.

****

****

Been enjoying your updates and photos. We are all thinking of you over there, easing the tension with the universal language of music.
Blessings your way.

****

I checked out your internet site, and I am very impressed. I love the idea of spreading peace through music---something I really believe in. I use music in my work as well, I work in mental health and use music, drumming, percussion whenever possible. I am always amazed at the results. I believe it opens the heart which is the source of all healing.

****

I am excited hearing about your travels. Thank you for sharing. I will share your emails with the handful of faculty and staff I work with here at the college. It is important that people here feel some sort of connection with the people from that area of the world.

****

I'm so glad you took the adventure and am even more glad that you have returned safely.
I loved your e-mails and photos. In fact, I wish you were still there and sending them.
Your heart-touching one-to-one musical ambassadorship makes so much sense. I'm sure that you and Kristina generated more understanding and goodwill than the entire U.S. government would even be able to do -- if they even cared. Your mission touched me and reminded me of an activist part of me that has been dormant for a long time. Your courage to face down the war machine inspires me.
Were you harrassed when you went through US customs?
Since you've been playing middle-eastern music for so long, it seemed poetically beautiful that you would take your passion and skill to the area that needs our compassion. I guess I'm a broken record here but I think that what you have done is fantastic.
You'll probably laugh, but I was concerned for your safety. We know that Bush is going to destroy the place and I wanted you to get out of there first. You did.
Sadly, US foreign policy is so neanderthal that huge parts of the world that would

116

be fascinating to visit will probably not be very welcoming to the ugly americans. Your music is your entry visa. The rest of us will have to experience vicariously through you. You're a good man, Cam. I enjoy my memories of you and love what you are doing now. Enclosed is a small contribution.
I love you.

****

I also spent quite a while reading the emails from your trip. It really opened my eyes about some things I did not know before.

****

You are utilizing the gift of music towards it's highest purpose, of spreading joy and building bridges towards peace, understanding and hope-in a way that transcends politics-

****

The thing that struck me about your presentation was the fact that the things I learned in school were so different than what your experiences showed these countries and people to be. I now know that it is safe to travel in the middle east, that I will not have my belongings stolen and that the people are generous and openhearted.

****

Your talents and skills are clearly appreciated there and your message of peace is shared by many around the world.

****

Your trip will be there with these people for the rest of their lives. I truly mean it. "The year when Kristina and Cameron were here."

****

What a beautiful and handsome people! Thanks for the photographs!

****

****

Cameron, the only words that come to mind are 'thankyou'. Thank you for going, thank you for sending back your wonderful chronicles. I find it very inspiring. Thank you! I look forward to every next installment.

Wow, you make these young people happy Therefore you deserve an award.

****

I have been very moved by your experience and look forward to continuing stories. So different from those we see and hear in the news every day. Peace.

****

It was so refreshing to hear your stories and your music coming in as a fresh breeze that begins the healing, the rebuilding, and the loving that just seems to flow so easily when music such as yours opens the heart...

****

I saw your interview on FSTV tonight, and now I know what you've been doing all these years. Singing is a wonderful connection to Spirit, in a way that spoken language can only hint at. Music surpasses the linearness of language, and is truly universal, even without multilingual capabilities.

I know you already know all that, but I wanted to let you know I really do understand.

I am learning that there is no us and them. We are all us. So when I saw what you were doing, I said hooray. There's lot's of hope left for this planet, in spite of our almost elected leadership.

I see you as an international Pete Seeger. I feel proud to have known you, way back when, and would be happy to re-connect.

****

You are both good souls. I hope and pray that others emulate your passion for peace, via music and paths of justice. God bless you both.

****

****

It is good to know you have returned safely!
I am envious of all of the positive influence and of all of the wonderful stories you have been involved in!

****

Getting your emails and hearing about your adventures just fill my heart. I so appreciate having both of you in my life.

****

I'm really enjoying your posts and have forwarded one of them to some 3000 people in my email lists.

****

Your stories are profound and wonderful--like a window open onto the world. I am so enjoying these installments of your time in Jordan, and the photos. Thank you for your thoughtful perspective and thorough consideration of the culture and people you encounter. Thank you for being there as emissaries of peace and love. And thank you for sharing with us the peace and love you are receiving there.

****

Re: Cameron & Kristina:
They do have balls! That's so great. Hopefully something such as this can make some difference at some level.

****

Very powerful descriptions and photos! I showed them to a Jordanian grad student/ friend of mine and he was happy, also surprised that you were hoping to visit Iraq, and of course impressed with the connection you are making with the people.

****

****

I am loving hearing from you on your trip. It gives me such hope and comfort that the ways of peace are active in the world. Thank you both.

****

I enjoy reading your feelings that are poured on paper (e-mail). I enjoy them specially because I know the places and also the faces and attitude are familiar. Just keep doing what you do but add questions to what you see. Solutions are different. Questions are more important and also more challenging.
The Middle East could be a better place. People could be more relaxed and hope could make their life better. Richness in not my concern. They need more of that thing, hope. What you see is not what is. Try to talk to these people and ask them questions regarding their plans for the future. What will they tell you about their future?
Boulder will be a great place where you process your information, later. It will take you time to understand even why you went there.

****

Your missives are being read avidly by many of us here. This afternoon we were singing peace songs. We send you Love and Light, and I've been especially interested to hear Kristina's impressions, as I know that the culture there is very different for women.

****

Be safe and, inch Allah, your impact will be greater than you'll ever know. You are both in my prayers. Thank you for the updates. They are very interesting. I'm sure you are dispelling myths on both sides of the Atlantic (and both sides need that bit of tolerance and acceptance of differences). We'll never agree, share all of the same values or see eye to eye but we must share the planet well in order to all live well.
----Your stateside-Egyptian-armchair traveler.

****

****

This sounds so wonderful. I am so proud of both of you and would love to meet you, Kristina. You are absolutely living your love and commitment to peace. Thanksgiving. Please keep sending the updates, and stay safe.

****

Thank you so much for all you have both done and continue to do. Receiving your emails has meant a lot to me and my family, so much so that I was cherishing them all in a folder in my computer. I have been studying Middle Eastern dancing and one of my teachers was just recently diagnosed with cancer. She and I were talking one day about your wonderful adventures, aspirations and experiences. She is quite interested in reading the emails.
Your work has brought tears to my eyes so many times along with the deepest of convictions that I know you have done the world a great service.

****

Just want to tell you how happy I am that you're now actively exploring your vision, feeling it, smelling it, tasting it, hearing it and singing it.
Please, please give our greetings to those you meet -- asalaamu aleikum wa rah-matullah wa barakatuhu (if you don't know this whole greeting, I'm sure they'll tell you its meaning, inshaA'llah). Please tell them of the Muslims in Abiquiu, NM, a small village w/ mud houses and wood stoves. We send to them our warm 'Eid Greetings and share our happiness to have fasted another month of Ramadan.

****

Thanks so much for your messages, it is wonderful to know that you are doing this and please tell people again that there are many of us behind what you are doing specifically and many generally who want peace, music, and don't believe in the destructiveness of what the US government is doing. We have so much better to offer. Thanks so much, and please don't worry about offending anyone, the truth is the truth. Thanks again for all you both are doing, and safe travels, may the creator watch over you and may you have wonderful and heart-touching experiences.

****

****

I am really enjoying the story of your trip. I want you to know that I am very proud of what you are doing, and my heart is with you. I will make a point of meeting you some day.

****

Hello- I just returned a week ago from a month in the Sahara desert- Niger & Algeria. What a surprise to find your stories continuing to reflect my experiences in some small way. It is a difficult return for me, as usual, to balance the equation of these different worlds - those of the Touareg nomads we visited, living simply of course, keeping their camels, goats, sheep, and observing the karem for Ramadan. The men mysterious, veiled and gowned - from a noble past. I sat one evening in the room of a young man who played the guitar for us (a now traditional instrument for them), a room with walls of mud & straw and dirt floor surrounded wall to wall by similar rooms and larger compounds in their small village. It was peaceful, gentle. They made tea for my friend and I and we enjoyed their performance for us. I love this part of the world; I've visited Morocco many times, and now I've gone onward, into more of it. There really is no way to explain that world to those who have never left the USA, except with simple images of the market place or the call to prayer, as you have done. Such a haunting song; sometimes I think I hear it in the distance.
Anyway, enough of my musings. Bon voyage and the best of luck to you both, and, insha'Allah, I will meet you sometime....

****

Thanks

Thanks to Kristina Sophia for endless spiritual inspiration and loving partnership.

Thanks to our kids, Loren, Melina and Lauren for their love and understanding.

Thanks to so many friends from Mexico to Baghdad who have lovingly adjusted our feathers for the duration of our Musical Mission of Peace and especially to those who have helped produce our "Singing in Baghdad" multimedia presentation across America.

Thanks to the musicians from California to Cairo who have patiently and lovingly offered their Arabic musical souls to help us learn so many lovely tunes and emotions and acquire little baby Arabic souls of our own.

Thanks to those millions whose stories, sometimes painful, remain untold.

Thanks to all for every personal suspension of negative judgment so that we can all grow in harmony.

Thanks to Zia Parker, Brooke Anderson and Vicki Londerville for their editing help.

For more info go to: http://www.musicalmissions.com

To donate to Musical Missions of Peace (a non-profit corporation), go to: http://www.musicalmissions.com/subscriptions.html

Cameron Powers
Biography

Fascination with Peruvian Indian peoples encountered on mountaineering expeditions led Cameron to spend eight years traveling to Andean villages in the 1960's and 70's. He immediately discovered the value of learning to play their music with them as an easy aid to bonding in trust and friendship.

Cameron graduated with a B.A. in Anthropology and Linguistics from the University of Colorado, Boulder, with an emphasis on the study of Quechua, the language of the Incas. He also received a fellowship to attend a two-month intensive immersion program in Quechua at Cornell University. It was there that he began to realize the value of being a musician as well as a linguist. Cameron also received a scholarship to work on a Doctoral program in Linguistics at the University of California, Berkeley. There he continued to study Quechua and began studies of the Tibetan language. In 1973 Cameron lived in Greece and studied Greek language and music.

Returning to Boulder, Cameron performed Greek music and began the study of Arabic music with local bands: "The Silk Route," "The Boulder Bouzouki Band," and "Solspice." He created musical instruments, houses, and Spanish language teaching programs in Boulder while raising his children. He began performing Middle Eastern and Balkan music with "Sherefe" in Boulder and traveled with the band to New Mexico and California for additional performances and studies.

Cameron has been associated since 1986 with the Middle Eastern Music Camp, which takes place every summer in Mendocino, California. He has studied at the Arabic Music Retreat in Mt. Holyoke, Massachusetts and with numerous musicians whom he has met on travels in Turkey, Syria, Jordan, Egypt and Morocco.

After the events of 9/11, a pall was cast on his role as an American playing Middle Eastern music. "Terrorism" had somehow entered the music. Performances were cancelled; people became nervous about producing Middle Eastern musical shows. From his travels in the Middle East and from his extensive chain of friendships with Middle Eastern musicians, Cameron knew a warm reception was available to anyone, including Americans, wishing to travel the Arab world. He realized the importance of continuing his "musical missions."

Recently back from Iraq, Egypt, Jordan, Syria, Lebanon and Palestine, Cameron and his partner, Kristina Sophia, are furthering opportunities to help people understand the Arabic psyche.

Other Books by Cameron Powers

Spiritual Traveler: Journeys Beyond Fear

ISBN: 978-0-9745882-1-6
Price: $16.95 (plus $4 shipping and handling)

If *Singing in Baghdad* captures your imagination and ignites in you a desire to learn more about the Arab world and psyche, you can delve further into this fascinating culture with *Spiritual Traveler: Journeys Beyond Fear.* This inspirational book is an in-depth exploration of the process of opening one's heart and soul to the realities of another culture. Who would guess that it's necessary to strip oneself naked and throw away every last system of belief, even some of those held most dear, in order to truly be ready to learn?

This book describes this process and reveals some of the rewards which await one who becomes an open pathway for learning. Awareness of telepathic communications and access to new levels of spontaneity are part of the rewards available to the non-judgemental mind. Did you know that Americans are nouns while Arabs are verbs? What does this mean? Did you realize that *the very meaning of life itself* completely shifts when you cross from one family of languages to another? This is why so many things are literally 'untranslatable!'

Musicians have long held many of the keys to cross-cultural journeying as a spiritual path. Because the author is a musician who has taken the time and trouble to first learn and then fall in love with Arabic music, techniques are described for entering into adventures beyond words. In this book we find many clues about Arab-world people and the beauty of their ancient ways. With fear removed from our perceptions, we find the way paved for endless cross-cultural love affairs. We learn some of the seemingly magical formulas for understanding other people across ancient, tribal boundaries as well as modern national borders.

126

Arabic Musical Scales: Basic Maqam Teachings

Book and two audio CDs
ISBN: 978-0-9745882-3-0
Price: $34.95 (plus $4 shipping and handling)

This comprehensive book and CD set includes 45 scales for the musician interested
in learning to play Near Eastern dance music, sacred music, or folk music.

From Cairo to Tunisia, Damascus to
Baghdad, Beirut to Aleppo, and as far west
as Istanbul and Greece, musicians live and
breathe these ancient scales, which have
survived intact for hundreds, and in some
cases, thousands of years.

Anyone interested in micro-tonal musical
intervals would do well to dip into this ancient tradition.

Additional copies of *Singing in Baghdad*
or the books listed above can be ordered at:

Website: http://www.gldesignpub.com
or E-Mail: distrib@gldesign.com

Or send check of money order to:
GL Design
2090 Grape Ave
Boulder, CO 80304   USA

For more information visit: http://www.musicalmissions.com

Printed in the United States
42820LVS00003B/181-330

9 780974 588254